BEATRIX POTTER

Artist, Storyteller and Countrywoman

BEATRIX POTTER

Artist, Storyteller and Countrywoman

JUDY TAYLOR

FREDERICK WARNE

FREDERICK WARNE
Penguin Books Ltd, 27 Wrights Lane, London W8 5TZ (Publishing and Editorial)
and Harmondsworth, Middlesex, England (Distribution and Warehouse)
Viking Penguin Inc., 40 West 23rd Street, New York, New York, 10010, U.S.A.
Penguin Books Australia Ltd, Ringwood, Victoria, Australia
Penguin Books Canada Limited, 2801 John Street, Markham, Ontario, Canada L3R 1B4
Penguin Books (N.Z.) Ltd, 182–190 Wairau Road, Auckland 10, New Zealand

First published 1986
Reprinted, with amendments, 1987

Designed by Gail Engert

ISBN 0 7232 3314 4

Set in Monophoto Sabon by Eta Services (Typesetters) Limited, Beccles, Suffolk

Printed and bound in Great Britain by William Clowes Limited, Beccles and London

British Library Cataloguing in Publication Data
    Taylor, Judy
        Beatrix Potter: artist, storyteller and countrywoman.
        1. Potter, Beatrix—Biography   2. Authors,
        English—20th century—Biography
        I. Title
        823'.912   PR6031.072Z/

        ISBN 0–7232–3314–4

Library of Congress catalog card number: 86-50799

PLATE I (*half-title*) Benjamin Bunny at Heath Park, Birnam,
where the Potters spent the summer of 1892

PLATE II (*frontispiece*) Some characters from 'the little books'

Contents

For my mother

List of colour plates

The page numbers given are those opposite the colour plates, or, in the case of a double-page spread, those either side of the plate

2 Bolton Gardens
Feb 3rd 05

Dear Mr Warne,

I had concluded you were still away & I will come next Thursday afternoon; I shall get the wall papers done by that time. I am making a copy in a different colour of one of them.

I wonder if you will care for either of these, don't bother to read them before hand if you are busy. There is plenty of work to go on with; though I don't intend to finish the hedgehog book straight off, as I think I may have a chance of drawing a child conveniently later in the spring.

I shall be very glad to get my drawings looked over.

With kind regards believe me yrs sincerely

Beatrix Potter

N. D. Warne Esq
15 Bedford St

I'm afraid you don't like *frogs* but it would make pretty pictures with water-forget-me-nots, lilies etc.

I should like to do both & I think I could, if the longer one were part black & white which takes very little time to process.

I don't know what to think about the second; it seems rather funny, but *very greedy*!

There is one thing in its favour, children like conversations.

Foreword

Beatrix Potter and her books have been part of my life for a long time. My first encounter, like that of so many others, was on my mother's lap, and I can hear her voice now reading *Mrs Tiggy-winkle* to me; it has remained my favourite of all the books.

How I wish I had known that Beatrix Potter was still alive when, as an eight-year-old, I was sent to boarding school in the Lake District at the beginning of the war. I should most certainly have found an excuse to call at Castle Cottage on one of those interminable and wide-ranging walks that took up every Saturday.

When I was a teenager and doing my share of child-minding, it was the time of post-war paper shortage, and the only readily available copies of Beatrix Potter's books were in French. Although she was 'Poupette-à-L'Epingle' on the page, Mrs Tiggy-winkle quickly reverted to her old self when read aloud.

Some years later, when I was editing and publishing for children, Beatrix Potter's books were a standard against which to measure everything new. Her uninhibited choice of words, her exquisite watercolours, her perfect marriage of text and illustration have inspired many a young writer and artist to produce their best.

There is by now quite a library of books about Beatrix Potter, and no doubt there will be many more for she was an intriguingly fascinating woman, but the first of them all, the one that drew attention to the person behind the books, was Margaret Lane's *The Tale of Beatrix Potter*, published in 1946. Like many people before me, that book was my springboard and to Margaret Lane I offer my thanks.

I have been given unrestricted access to the Frederick Warne archives, which include fascinating files of correspondence between the company and Beatrix Potter spanning over fifty years, from their first rejection of her sketches in November 1891 to her request, in July 1943, for more copies of her books, as she had given away all she had left as prizes to a party of Girl Guides. I have used Beatrix Potter's own words (and her, at times, eccentric spelling) to tell her own story wherever possible, and unless otherwise attributed all the quotations in this book are taken from her letters or from her journal.

In parallel with working on this book I have begun a collection of Beatrix Potter's letters for eventual selection and publication, many of the letters coming from widely separated parts of the world, precious possessions handed from one generation to another. In working on both books I have met many people who knew Beatrix, who remember stories and anecdotes about her and who have photographs of her and of her family. I am grateful to them all for making everything so readily available to me. I have also discovered how generous Beatrix Potter enthusiasts and specialists are with their knowledge, never hesitating to share their research or to suggest a new contact. I should like to thank in particular Mary Burkett of Abbot Hall Art Gallery, Winifred Boultbee, Barbara Cartland, John Clegg, Bryan Dawson, Joan Duke, David King of the Free Library of Philadelphia, Nicholas Garland, Cynthia Forbes of the Girl Guides Association, Mollie Green, Beatrix Hammarling, Betty Hart, John Heelis, Anne Hobbs of the Victoria and Albert Museum, Jean Holland, Patricia C. Lord, Jane Crowell Morse, Susan Denyer of the National Trust, Valerie Wingfield of the New York Public Library, Mary Noble, Robin Rodger of the Perth Museum and Art Gallery, Barbara Poulson of the Pierpoint Morgan Library, Rosalind Rawnsley, Conrad Rawnsley, Louisa Rhodes, Posy Simmonds, Tom Smith, Tom Storey, Willow Taylor, Joan Thornley, Margaret Maloney of the Toronto Public Library, and Irene Whalley. My special thanks to Nicholas Sargeant and Derrick Witty for their help with the photographs, to Gail Engert who did so much more than design the book, to Sue Hibbert for her index, and to Jackie Gumpert for her hours of typing.

chapter one

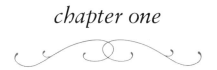

'My brother and I were born in London
because my father was a lawyer there.'

Beatrix with her brother, Bertram, in November 1878

On Saturday, the 28th inst. at 2 Bolton-gardens,
South Kensington, the wife of RUPERT POTTER, Esq.,
barrister-at-law, of a daughter.

THE ANNOUNCEMENT of the safe delivery of Helen Beatrix
Potter appeared in *The Times* of Monday, 30 July 1866. On
the same day the paper reported the deaths of over sixty
people 'in or nearby Llanelly' of cholera – and the opening to the
public of the recently completed Atlantic Cable between Europe
and America. Madame Tussauds advertised an addition to their
exhibition of the marriage group of their Royal Highnesses Prin-
cess Helena and Prince Christian; the Middlesex County Lunatic
Asylum in Colney-hatch offered a salary of £30 a year for a female
head attendant; and the large London shops announced 'the
inauguration of Saturday Half Holidays, closing their doors at
Two o'clock'. Political agitation was in the air, the trade unions
becoming daily more strident in their demands for wage increases,

Bolton Gardens, the square in
London where Beatrix was
born on 28 July 1866.
Photographed by Rupert Potter
in 1889.

with large open-air marches in London to draw attention to their case. There was active American support for the unrest in Ireland as the campaign grew for the repeal of the Act of Union; and there were signs that the cattle plague that had been raging through the country was at last beginning to wane.

'My brother and I were born in London because my father was a lawyer there,' wrote Beatrix Potter some seventy-five years later. 'But our descent – our interests and our joy was in the north country.' And that was indeed the case. Beatrix and Bertram's grandparents on both sides of the family were Lancashire born and bred, and both families had made their fortunes out of cotton.

Their great-grandfather was a cotton merchant, but their grandfather, Edmund Potter, at the age of twenty-three, decided to follow in his uncle's footsteps and to specialise in calico printing. In 1824 he set up in partnership with his cousin, Charles, in Dinting Vale near Glossop, east of Manchester, where they took over an old mill and patterned the rough grey calico with coloured dyes applied by hand-printed wood-blocks. It was a difficult time.

'We started in a humble way,' wrote Edmund, 'but our textures eventually took a good position in the market and we got on. We soon found that we had entered into a very severe struggle and on naturally looking about for the cause of it discovered that we had entered into a trade that was more severely taxed than any other.'

The tax Edmund was referring to was print duty, and it was his concern about what he saw as the iniquities of print duty that started his lifelong interest in politics, for in 1830 he joined a delegation of printers and cotton manufacturers which journeyed to London to petition the Government to repeal the tax that was killing their business. Although their petition was successful and the tax was abolished the following year, it was not in time to save the firm to which Edmund and Charles were allied, and Potter's Printworks failed. But Edmund Potter was not one to be beaten by adversity, and he started up his calico business all over again while cousin Charles 'branched off into wallpaper'.

Edmund was an enlightened employer. He cared about the standard of work that came from Edmund Potter and Company and he cared about the men he employed to do it. He replaced the time-consuming method of hand-block printing with the new-fangled machine printing, and he built a library and reading room for his workers. As was common practice in the nineteenth century, he employed child workers, and across from the works he built for them a day school, which they shared with the children of the other employers. A dining-room in the works provided everyone with cheap food, and for efficiency and economy Edmund Potter took a lease on a local farm especially for the purpose. By 1845 Edmund Potter and Company was a vast printworks, with its own

Edmund Potter (1802–83), Beatrix's paternal grandfather, was a Unitarian and the owner of a vast calico printing works in Glossop, near Manchester. He was elected Liberal M.P. for Carlisle in 1861.

Edmund Potter looked after his workers well, providing them with a reading room and library (*above*) as well as a school.

(*right*) Edmund Potter and Company had its own private reservoirs, over which the Dinting Arches viaduct carried the first train in December 1845.

(*below left*) John Bright (1811–89) was a frequent visitor to the Potter household. First elected to Parliament in 1843, he fought with Cobden for the repeal of the Corn Laws.

(*below right*) Richard Cobden (1804–65) was also a close friend of Edmund Potter. He entered Parliament in 1841 and was a leader of the Anti-Corn Law League.

reservoirs over which the magnificent Dinting Arches viaduct carried the trains from Gamesley to Woodhead. It was the world's largest calico printworks, and Potter prints were world-famous.

Edmund Potter was a strong Unitarian, as was his wife, Jessie Crompton, whom he had married in 1829. She was regarded as something of a beauty, the daughter of a property owner in Lancashire and the Lake District from whom she had inherited her somewhat unusual non-conformist and radical views. The Potters' home in Manchester was a busy place. Their seven children, four boys and three girls, were born in the first eleven years of their marriage; their second son, Rupert, in 1832. When their fortunes improved, the Potters entertained generously, and among

Edmund's many friends were the two men who were to change the course of his life and to bring the Potters south, Richard Cobden and John Bright – and again it was cotton that had brought Potter and Cobden together. Cobden started his working life as a traveller for a London calico merchant and by 1831 he was a partner in a Lancashire calico factory. Bright, a Quaker and the son of a Rochdale miller, was deeply involved, together with Cobden, with the Anti-Corn Law League, campaigning tirelessly for the repeal of the Corn Laws which gave protection to farmers for their corn prices. In 1841 Cobden was elected M.P. for Stockport, and two years later Bright was elected M.P. for Durham, the start of two political careers with far-reaching importance. The conversation in the Potter household was inevitably strongly political.

In 1842 Edmund Potter moved his family from Manchester to be near the printworks. He had built a large and elegant house, Dinting Lodge, overlooking the reservoirs, and now he could entertain his friends in rather more luxury. They journeyed the twelve miles from Manchester to Dinting on the new-fangled railway or drove in their carriages, bumping and clattering through the countryside. Among those who made the journey were the Gaskells, William who was joint minister of Cross Street Chapel, and Elizabeth his wife, not yet embarked upon her writing career. Every summer, for their holidays, the Potters took a large house in Scotland, and William Gaskell was a regular guest there, too.

The Manchester School of Art, of which Edmund Potter was President from 1855 to 1858, a direct consequence of his involvement in the training of textile designers.

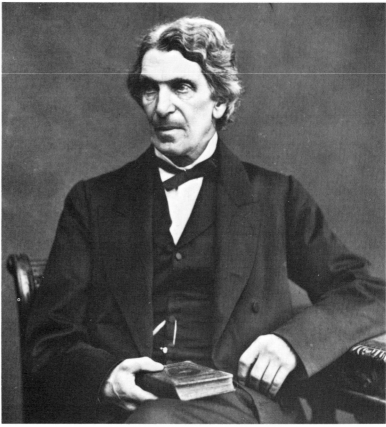

James Martineau (1805–1900),
a Unitarian pastor, was
professor at Manchester New
College where he taught the
young Rupert Potter, Edmund's
second son.

By now Edmund Potter was a very successful businessman. He was President of the Chamber of Commerce and President of the Manchester School of Art, the latter a direct consequence of his involvement in the training of textile designers, and his achievements in the scientific printing of calico had been crowned by a Fellowship of the Royal Society. The printworks was flourishing and his eldest son, Crompton, was taking a responsible part in the management of the business. The time had come for Edmund to recognise an ambition he had had for many years – to stand for Parliament. In 1861 Edmund Potter was elected Liberal member for Carlisle, and that same year he left Manchester for London.

The Potters' second son, Rupert, after attending local schools with his brother, had been sent at sixteen to the Unitarian Manchester New College. Among his teachers were William Gaskell and James Martineau, Harriet's younger brother, both of whom had a strong influence on him. Many years later Beatrix Potter recorded a meeting between the old Dr Martineau and his erstwhile pupil: 'I think Papa has a greater respect and admiration for Dr Martineau as to his intellect and character than any other man.

I have heard him say he is the only man to whom he would trust his conscience implicitly in religious matters, as having a certain reliance on his clearness and good sense.'

Rupert was a good student and was awarded prizes for classics and ancient history. He also studied mathematics, physics, French and German and was awarded his B.A. in 1851, the first in the family to achieve such distinction.

It was expected that Rupert would now join the family business in which his brother was already hard at work, but he had set his heart on becoming a barrister. So early in 1854, Rupert went to London as a student of law at Lincoln's Inn, a strange contrast to his life in rural Glossop. The work was hard and the hours of study long but Rupert did well, alleviating the pressure by sketching. He had always been interested in drawing, and his sketchbook of that time is full of meticulous drawings of birds and animals, contrasting with his caricatures of both men and animals drawn with considerable humour.

On 17 November 1857, Rupert Potter was called to the Bar. He was twenty-five years old and embarking upon a career as different

Rupert Potter kept a sketchbook while studying law at Lincoln's Inn in the mid 1850s. Fifty years later his daughter was also to draw a duck in a bonnet.

Rupert Potter was called to the bar in 1857 and in 1863 he married Helen Leech, the daughter of a prosperous Lancashire cotton merchant.

to that of his brothers as could be imagined. His specialisation was as an equity draughtsman and conveyancer, with Chambers in Lincoln's Inn for three years and at No. 3 New Square for the next thirty years.

When Rupert was thirty-one he married Helen, one of the daughters of John Leech, an old Unitarian friend of the Potters, a prosperous cotton merchant from Stalybridge and a colourful character. John Leech was full of ideas to increase his business and earned himself the reputation of 'the cutest man on the Manchester Royal Exchange'. In order to save paying money to others for the importing of raw cotton, he had built his own ships and thus became a shipbuilder as well as a cotton merchant. He was married to Jane Ashton, whose family came from Dukinfield in Greater Manchester. On their wedding day the bridegroom's clothes were 'very tight-fitting' and they 'drove all over England for their wedding tour in a chariot, and it was the nicest journey she ever went'. John Leech was 'rather fond of fine phrases. Once when he went to London for the day, he told all his friends he was a "bird of prey", meaning to say "passage".'

Like many of the prosperous families of the day, the Leechs had a large brood of children, five daughters and three sons. Their fifth

PLATE III (above) A page from the drawing book that nine-year-old Beatrix made on holiday at Dalguise in 1875.

PLATE IV (left) Harebells and marguerites painted by Beatrix in July 1880, when she was nearly fourteen.

PLATE V (left) Beatrix and her brother, Bertram, kept bats as pets. This one was recorded by Beatrix in April 1887.

PLATE VI (below) A privet hawk-moth, caterpillar and chrysalis (actual size) and a highly magnified section of wing-scales, February 1887.

child, Elizabeth, married Walter Potter, Rupert's younger brother, and on 8 August 1863, two years after her father's death, Helen married Rupert Potter in the Unitarian chapel in Hyde, near Manchester. She was twenty-four, seven years younger than her husband and in possession of a good legacy from her father.

For the first three years of their married life the Potters lived in Upper Harley Street, a fashionable part of London at the time, not closely associated with the medical profession as it is today. When Helen was expecting their first child they moved to Bolton Gardens, a square of newly-built, four-storeyed houses in the peace and quiet of rural Kensington. No. 2 Bolton Gardens was to remain their home until Rupert's death nearly fifty years later.

For a house of such size Mrs Potter needed a number of servants, and she engaged two sisters from Stalybridge, Elizabeth and Sarah Harper, Sarah to look after the cooking and Elizabeth to supervise the housekeeping. Then there was George Cox, 'a starched London butler, a man excelling in the setting-up of cocked-hat table napkins, immaculate silver and precision of cutlery', a coachman called Reynolds and a groom to care for the carriage horses stabled in Bolton Garden Mews. When Helen Beatrix was born, a nurse was added to the retinue.

The third-floor nursery in Bolton Gardens was for the next forty-seven years Beatrix's playroom, schoolroom and eventually her studio. Much has been written about the strictness of her childhood, but the Potters were no more overbearing than any other middle-class parents of the time. Children were seen and not

The view from the garden of No. 2 Bolton Gardens photographed by Rupert Potter in April 1890. The Potters had moved to their new house in 1866 when Helen was expecting their first child, Beatrix.

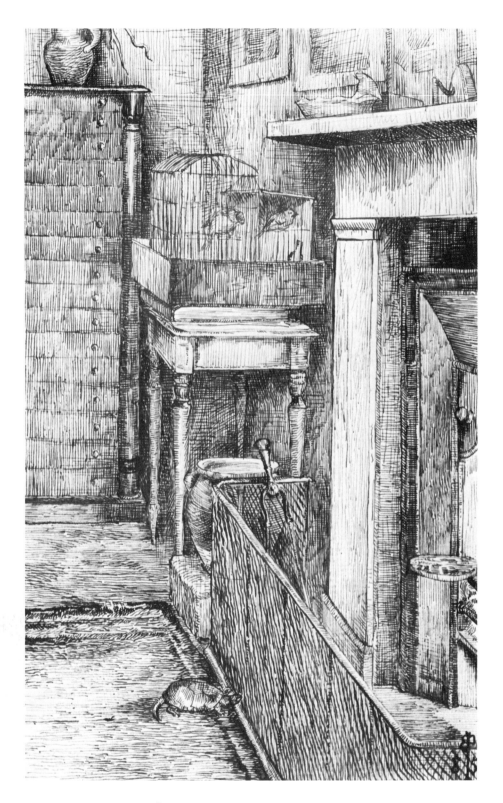

heard; they were looked after almost exclusively by their nannies and governesses and were brought downstairs to see their parents only on special occasions or to say goodnight. Occasionally Mrs Potter would climb the long staircase to the nursery, but it was a rare occurrence and much went on there that she knew nothing about. It was, after all, 'nanny's kingdom'.

Beatrix's nurse was a young woman from the Highlands of Scotland, where the Potters went for their holiday every summer. 'She had a firm belief in witches, fairies and the creed of the terrible John Calvin (the creed rubbed off but the fairies remained) ... I can remember quite plainly from one to two years old; not only facts, like learning to walk but places and sentiments ... I only cared for two toys; a dilapidated black wooden doll called Topsy,

(*opposite*) A corner of the third-floor schoolroom at No. 2 Bolton Gardens, drawn by Beatrix in 1885 when she was nineteen.

Rupert Potter was a keen photographer and his wife and daughter frequently sat for him.

Beatrix, wearing her 'cotton stockings striped round like zebra's legs', was photographed at Dalguise with William Gaskell.

and a grimy, hard-stuffed, once-white, flannelette pig (which gradually parted with a tail made of tape). The pig did not belong to me. Grandmamma kept it in the bottom drawer of her *secrétaire*.'

Nurse McKenzie had sole charge of Beatrix and looked after her with strict and spartan attention. She fed her, dressed her, coaxed her to crawl and to walk, taught her her first words – and introduced her to fairies. The books Beatrix liked best were 'trash, from the literary point of view – goody goody, powder-in-the-jam, from the modern standpoint! I liked silly stories about other little girls' doings.' But her fairly sparse reading diet was marvellously mixed. 'I remember my nurse reading *Uncle Tom's Cabin* to me when I was a small child,' and when Beatrix began to read for herself, the Potter family library was her best source of reading material. 'I learned to read on the Waverly novels; I had had a horrid large print primer and a stodgy fat book – I think it was called a *History of the Robin Family* by Mrs Trimmer.* I know I hated it – then I

* It must have been *The History of the Robins*, for the instruction of children on their treatment of animals, Griffith & Farran, London, 1869.

was let loose on *Rob Roy*, and spelled through a few pages painfully; then I tried *Ivanhoe* – and *The Talisman* – then I tried *Rob Roy* again; all at once I began to READ (missing the long words, of course) ... I had very few books – Miss Edgworth and Scott's novels I read over and over.'

Beatrix was a delicate child and often ill. She knew few other children and seldom ventured out in London, except for walks in Kensington Gardens with her first dog, Sandy, a brown Scotch terrier, and with her nurse, who saw that she was carefully dressed. 'What I wore was absurdly uncomfortable; white *piqué* starched frocks just like Tenniel's *Alice in Wonderland*, and cotton stockings striped round like zebra's legs', with high black-buttoned boots. Her hair was worn brushed straight back and held in place by a plain band behind the ears, 'black velvet on Sundays, and either black or brown ribbon week days ... I remember the bands fastened with a bit of elastic, looped over a button behind the ear; it hurt.'

While young Beatrix was in the safe care of her nurse, Rupert Potter was enjoying the life of a gentleman in London, leaving his practice to be looked after by others. He visited his club, the Reform, where he felt at home among fellow Liberal sympathisers, particularly his father's old friend, John Bright. He discussed poetry with Lewis Morris, a fellow conveyancer, 'the poet laureate of lady's schools and respectability' and intimate of Lord Tennyson. He pursued his interest in art and painting, with regular visits to exhibitions at the Royal Academy or to art galleries to add to his growing collection of pictures, particularly the drawings of Randolph Caldecott. He continued the sketching and drawing that had seen him through his student days, but he was not a painter. Eighteen years later his daughter commented in her journal, 'I am

Two of Rupert Potter's drawings were reproduced on plates for the nursery at Bolton Gardens.

Beatrix recorded in her journal of 28 July 1884, 'Papa has been photographing old Gladstone this morning at Mr Millais'.'

sure he has not the least idea of the difficulty of painting a picture. He can draw very well, but he has hardly attempted water-colour, and never oil.' Rupert often took his wife to the theatre, expressing a preference for comedy and light opera, and he became more and more interested in photography, the relatively new art form that had caught his attention shortly before his marriage to Helen.

Photographic equipment in those days was cumbersome and heavy, but Rupert had servants to carry it, which enabled him to indulge often in his new enthusiasm, photographing the ever-changing scene of London's streets as well as his long-suffering family and friends. In 1869 he was elected as a member of the Photographic Society of London; now he could both contribute to and learn from their monthly journal, and exhibit in their annual exhibition. He became a skilled photographer, always remaining

Sir John Everett Millais'
portrait of 'The Right
Honourable W. E. Gladstone,
1885', for which Rupert Potter's
photograph was the reference.

an amateur but working closely with his friend, the painter John Everett Millais, sometimes providing landscape backgrounds for him to use in his portraits, at other times photographing his sitters for the artist's reference. Millais, who was married to John Ruskin's ex-wife, greatly widened the circle of Rupert Potter's acquaintance and brought him into contact with a variety of people, among them Lady Peggy Primrose, the youngest daughter of the Earl of Rosebery, and William Gladstone who was in his last year as prime minister. Rupert Potter was a meticulous photographer, seldom failing to note the place and date on the back of each photograph as soon as the print was dry and carefully storing them in big boxes and albums. His photographs remain a valuable record over a century later.

Helen Potter left behind the life of a country gentlewoman and

23

'Newton from near Tower, Gorse Hall', a water-colour by Beatrix's mother, Helen Leech, done in the more leisurely days before her marriage.

now spent her time keeping up the social responsibilities of a London lady. There was no longer an opportunity for indulging in her 'passable water colours'; instead she drove out in the carriage to leave her card or to sip tea with the other ladies of Kensington, returning to prepare herself for frequent elaborate dinner parties at No. 2 Bolton Gardens. Guests at the Potters for dinner did not leave hungry. On 7 May 1875, for instance, they dined on 'Spring Soup, Salmon, Sweetbreads, Lobster Cutlets, Spring Chickens, Ham, Roast Lamb, Ducklings and Peas, Mousseline Pudding, Jelly, Cherry Ice and Brown Bread Ice.'

When Helen Beatrix was nearly six, her brother Walter Bertram was born. She had been named after her mother, and Walter was given his uncle's name, and to avoid confusion both children were known by their second names, Beatrix and Bertram, and to their parents and close family friends as 'B' and 'Bertie'. Now that there were two children to engage the attention of the nurse, it was natural that the elder should find it even more necessary to make her own amusements. Beatrix had inherited her parents' artistic talents, and when at an early age she discovered the pleasure it gave her to draw and to paint, she was given every encouragement. She also began to take notice of the pictures in the books she was reading, and as she grew older her parents now saw to it that there was an increasing supply of new books in the nursery. 'I had Mrs Molesworth's as they came out, with the Walter Crane pictures', and Mrs Ewing's *The Brownies* which had pictures by

Cruikshank, as well as copies of the *St Nicholas* magazine which at that time featured the work of Reginald Birch and of the young Howard Pyle. 'Probably I was about six or seven ... when a friend of my father's, Professor Wilson, from Oxford came in and produced a book from his pocket and discussed with my Mother whether I was old enough or whether the book was too old? which was the same thing. It had been written by another Oxford don and was attracting attention. I became immediately so absorbed with Tenniel's illustrations that I don't remember what they said about Lewis Carroll.'

Beatrix saw her parents more frequently now she was getting older but she found her mother remote and not a little frightening. It was her father who was her favourite and with whom she had an increasingly close relationship. Often, when business or holidays

Beatrix began drawing at an early age and filled sketchbooks all her life. This is from a drawing book she kept at Dalguise when she was nine.

My dear Papa
      I am not
to go out in the
garden as I
have got a
cold. From

When they were apart Beatrix wrote to her father with the news. This letter is thought to have been written by her in 1875, when she was nine.

Camfield Place in Hertfordshire is today the home of Barbara Cartland, little changed from 1866 when Beatrix's grandfather, Edmund Potter, bought it for his retirement.

separated them, they wrote to each other with the news. 'Dear papa, I am not to go out in the garden as I have got a cold. From your aff H.B. Potter.' 'My dear B, I hope you will get rid of the cold as soon as you can. You will give it to Mama, I think. I am your Papa.'

In 1866, Beatrix's grandfather, Edmund Potter, had retired and moved with his wife from their house in Queen's Gate to Camfield Place in Hatfield, Hertfordshire, 'a good-sized small-roomed old house of no particular pretensions, the outside red brick, white-washed', but with a 300-acre estate and extensive gardens laid out by Capability Brown in 1800. It was paradise for London children and Beatrix adored it, 'the place I love best in the world ... the notes of the stable clock and the all pervading smell of new-mown hay, the distant sounds of the farmyard ... Can you not see in your mind's eye, as plainly as I am who am here, the windy north front on its terrace, with the oaks moaning and swaying on winter nights close to the bedroom windows, and at their feet the long green slope of meadow down to the ponds ... Further east, beyond the sweep of grass-land and scattered oaks, the blue distance opens out, rising to the horizon over Panshanger Woods. If you get on any rising ground in this neighbourhood you would fancy Hert-fordshire was one great oak wood. There are trees in every hedge-row, and, seen from the moderate elevation of our hills, they seem to stand one against another. In summer the distant landscapes are intensely blue ...

'Not less beautiful is the winter, when the oaks are clothed in a

delicate tracery of snow and hoar-frost, they sometimes look quite orange-coloured in the sunshine against the sky, and yet the hoar-frost scarcely drips. My grandmother says when it snows in Hertfordshire it lies all winter. Have you ever noticed what a peculiar blue the snow is during a white frost? I know no colour like it except that milky lemon-blue which you find in the seed of wild balsam. At such times of frost and snow the two great cedars on the lawn look their best. The snow lies in wreaths on their broad outstretched arms, or melting, trickles down the dusty green bark with red stains.'

And at Camfield there was the farm produce. 'There was something rapturous to us London children in the unlimited supply of new milk. I remember always the first teas of the visit when we were thirsty and tired. How I watched at the window for the little farm-boy, staggering along the carriage-drive with the cans! It came up warm in a great snuff-coloured jug which seemed to have no bottom, and made the milk look blue.

'I seem to hear the chink of the crockery as the nurse-girl brought it out of the closet in the wall and laid the coarse, clean

Beatrix was very fond of her father and would patiently pose with him while the delayed action camera did its work.

table cloth. I think the earthenware had a peculiar cool pleasant taste . . . Then we had eggs, so new that the most perverse kitchen-maid could not hard-boil them.'

But, above all, Camfield Place was inextricably linked for Beatrix with her grandmother. The young Beatrix used to sit on a cross bar under the library table nursing her precious flannelette pig, 'the table cloth had a yellowy green fringe, and Grandmamma also had very hard gingersnap biscuits in a canister. I remember one of my teeth (milk teeth) came out in consequence (on purpose?) while I was under the table.' Old Mrs Potter lent her granddaughter books – Miss Edgworth's *Simple Susan* 'in a little old dumpy edition' – and regaled her with tales of her own child-hood at Gorse Hall. The strong bond forged between grandmother and granddaughter lasted until Jessie Potter's death in 1891 at the age of ninety.

The journey to Camfield from London was not difficult and visits there were frequent. In addition the Potters left London for two weeks every April to stay in seaside hotels in the West Country, in Ilfracombe, Minehead, Falmouth or Sidmouth, and in the summer the entire household went away from the end of July until well into October. For the first eighteen years of his marriage Rupert Potter, like his father before him, took the family to his favourite Scotland for this long summer holiday, renting a large country house with an estate. For the summer of 1871 he arranged to lease Dalguise House, an elegant mansion overlooking the River Tay near Dunkeld in Perthshire, the property of Charles Stuart who had gone to live in South Africa where he had been made Master of the Supreme Court. Dalguise was the Potter summer home for the next eleven years, the family journeying north on the train from King's Cross for three months of country pursuits, the adults to shoot grouse and pheasants, to stalk the stag on the estate or to fish the Tay for salmon, the children joining in the fishing or going off on their own to explore the great river and its stony beaches or to run wild through the woods.

Dalguise was the perfect place for small London children, and the Scottish countryside influenced Beatrix and Bertram for the rest of their lives. It was a place of magic and enchantment. 'The woods were peopled by the mysterious good folk. The Lords and Ladies of the last century walked with me along the overgrown paths, and picked the old fashioned flowers among the box and rose hedges of the garden . . . I remember every stone, every tree, the scent of the heather, the music sweetest mortal ears can hear, the murmuring of the wind through the fir trees. Even when the thunder growled in the distance, and the wind swept up the valley in fitful gusts, oh, it was always beautiful, home sweet home . . . the sun sinking, showing, behind the mountains, the purple shadows

Beatrix posed with her governess, Miss Davidson, for this photograph by Rupert Potter, believed to have been taken in 1876.

H.B. Potter. Oct. 1877.

creeping down the ravines into the valley to meet the white mist rising from the river. Then, an hour or two later, the great harvest-moon rose over the hills, the fairies came out to dance on the smooth turf, the night-jar's eerie cry was heard, the hooting of the owls, the bat flitted round the house, roe-deer's bark sounded from the dark woods, and faint in the distance, then nearer and nearer came the strange wild music of the summer breeze.'

It was at Dalguise that Beatrix discovered with amazement and delight the wild life about her. When Bertram was old enough he joined his sister on her expeditions, tracking the shy and easily startled roe-deer or seeking out the wild flowers, to study them and above all to draw them. Beatrix spent much of her time drawing and painting. Examples of her work from that time show that she was already, at the age of eight and nine, showing promise. She drew everything, from the game that the grown-ups brought back after a day's shooting to the buttercups picked in the meadows. The children caught rabbits, tamed them, drew them and sometimes even took them back to London. They skinned dead rabbits and boiled them until only the bones were left; then they studied the skeletons, drew them and preserved them in their collection.

The long family holidays gave Beatrix ample time for drawing. This landscape is dated October 1877, when she was eleven.

29

They came to recognise the birds in the surrounding woods and fields, they identified their calls and knew where they built their nests – and in all their exploration and discovery Beatrix and Bertram were encouraged by their father.

'I remember so clearly – as clearly as the brightness of rich Scotch sunshine on the threadbare carpet – the morning I was ten years old – and my father gave me Mrs Blackburn's book of birds, drawn from nature, for my birthday present. I remember the dancing expectation and knocking at their bedroom door, it was a Sunday morning, before breakfast. I kept it in the drawing room cupboard, only to be taken out after I had washed my grimy little hands under that wonderful curved brass tap, which being lifted, let loose the full force of ice-cold amber-water from the hills. The book was bound in scarlet with a gilt edge. I danced about the house with pride, never palled.' And the local people knew of their interest in wild life and often added to their collection. 'I shall never forget old Mr Wood coming to Dalguise one hot Monday afternoon in search of "worms", and producing a present out of his hat of about two dozen buff-tip caterpillars, collected on the road. They ought to have been in a red cotton pocket handkerchief, but they had got loose amongst his venerable grey locks.'

Rupert Potter invited his friends from London to join in the fun at Dalguise. Millais came to indulge his passion for fishing, bringing with him his wife and daughters; John Bright, another keen fisherman, spent many a happy time there and was a great favourite with the children; but Beatrix's dearest friend, William Gaskell, now a widower and in his early seventies, came often. When she was eight, Beatrix knitted him a comforter as a Christmas present which pleased him greatly; '... every time I put it round my neck – which during this weather will be every day – I shall be sure to think of you.'

William Gaskell loved being with the children and shared their joy in their love of animals. After one of his holidays at Dalguise, when he had left to stay elsewhere in Scotland, he wrote to Beatrix: 'A rabbit lying among the heather reminded me of Tommy, who I hope is taking his food properly, and doing well. If you think he remembers me, please give him my kind regards.'

After Gaskell's death, ten years later, Beatrix recalled one of the Scottish holidays they shared. 'Oh how plainly I see it again. He is sitting comfortably in the warm sunshine on the doorstep at Dalguise, in his grey coat and old felt hat. The newspaper lies on his knees, suddenly he looks up with his gentle smile. There are sounds of pounding footsteps. The blue-bottles whizz off the path. A little girl in a print frock and striped stockings bounds to his side and offers him a bunch of meadowsweet. He just says "thank you, dear", and puts his arm round her.

The young Beatrix particularly enjoyed drawing flowers and always brought back something to draw from country walks.

30

'The bees hum round the flowers, the air is laden with the smell of roses, Sandy lies in his accustomed place against the doorstep. Now and then a party of swallows cross the lawn and over the house, screaming shrilly, and the deep low of the cattle comes answering one another across the valley, borne on the summer breeze which sweeps down through the woods from the heathery moors.'

At Dalguise, as in London or wherever they happened to be, Rupert Potter photographed everyone and everything, his guests with their day's catch, Beatrix and Bertram with their governess, the house in its impressive setting.

The Bolton Gardens servants travelled to Scotland, too, some going on ahead to prepare the house, the others travelling with the family. The Harper sisters from Stalybridge were glad to be in the

(*above left*) The Potters took Dalguise House, near Dunkeld, for the summer from 1871–81 and the Millais family were frequent visitors. Rupert Potter titled his photograph 'After the salmon fishing'.

(*above right*) Beatrix in her 'hair band which hurt' with her dear friend, William Gaskell, in Scotland.

When Beatrix was twelve a Miss Cameron was appointed to teach her drawing. This rather stiff crayon drawing was done the following year, in December 1879.

Left on her own Beatrix drew with much more freedom. This sketch was inscribed: 'Siskin, who died August 20th 1879 at Dalguise'.

country again and they all welcomed the company of those employed on the estate. After only her second visit to Dalguise, Sarah the cook stayed in Scotland to marry the gamekeeper, Mr McDonald.

The return to London after the long months in the country, where lessons took second place to outings and expeditions, also meant a return to more serious work for the children. The nursery had been turned into the schoolroom when Beatrix's first govern-ess, Miss Hammond, came to start her education, and as soon as Bertram was old enough he joined in the lessons. As well as the basic 'reading, writing and arithmetic' a generous portion of their timetable was allocated to painting and drawing, and when Beatrix was twelve a Miss Cameron was engaged specifically to teach drawing. 'I have great reason to be grateful to her, though we were not on particularly good terms for the last good while. I have learnt from her freehand, model, geometry, perspective and a little water-colour flower painting. Painting is an awkward thing to teach except the details of the medium. If you and your master are determined to look at nature and art in two different directions you are sure to stick.'

Beatrix seldom drew people and never drew them well, but she drew and painted everything else: the garden at Bolton Gardens, the cliffs at Tenby, the farm buildings at Camfield Place; she copied illustrations from the books she was reading, she drew the vases of flowers on the table in the schoolroom, the fruit in the dining-room, and above all she painted in meticulous detail the

flowers and animals that she and Bertram had brought back from Dalguise on their various expeditions, or had bought in pet shops in London. The animals had to be kept upstairs in the schoolroom and smuggled down to the garden for the occasional airing. There was a green frog called Punch, two lizards Toby and Judy, some water newts, and a particular treasure called Sally that they bought in Hertfordshire: 'Yesterday, we bought a little ring-snake four-teen inches long, it was so pretty. It hissed like fun and tied itself into knots in the road when it found it could not escape, but did not attempt to bite as the blind worms do. It smelled strongly when in the open road, but not unpleasantly. Blind worms smell like very salt shrimps gone bad ... [The following day] – A day of misfortunes. Sally and four black newts escaped overnight. Caught one black newt in school room and another in larder, but nothing seen of poor Sally, who is probably sporting outside somewhere.'

During the years that Miss Cameron taught art in the Potter household the range of Beatrix's other lessons broadened consider-ably and she was gently encouraged to take an interest in wider issues. As well as keenly supporting Beatrix's own artistic activi-ties, her father began to take her with him to exhibitions and art galleries. He discussed politics and the affairs of the day with her, allowed her to listen in to the inevitable political discussions that raged around the Potter dinner table, and sometimes she accom-panied him on his visits to Mr Millais's studio where the painter gave her advice on how to mix her paints. But what Beatrix really missed at this time of her life was a friend, someone other than her

Rupert Potter sometimes took Beatrix with him to Millais' studio, where she was given advice on how to mix her paints.

Bertram was six years younger than Beatrix but shared her keen interest in animals and in drawing.

brother – of whom she was extremely fond and with whom she shared much but to whom she could hardly pour out her heart. She needed someone to discuss things with and to comment on the daily routine. Beatrix's relationship with her mother was growing more difficult every day, and both her parents had always discouraged their children in close friendships with others, fearing exposure to germs and bad influences. The substitute for human companionship for Beatrix were her pets – and a diary, kept in paper-covered exercise books with ruled pages and on loose sheets of paper. To ensure that her journal was kept secret from prying eyes, particularly her mother's, Beatrix invented a code. Though basically a simple substitution of letter for letter, it became so easy for her to use that she made her entries in a flowing script which remained undeciphered for over eighty years, until a dedicated Potter specialist and collector, Leslie Linder, finally broke the code in 1958. Even Beatrix herself found it impossible to read later in her life. 'I used to write long winded descriptions, hymns(!) and records of conversations in a kind of cypher shorthand, which I am now unable to read even with a magnifying glass.'

The journal is full of descriptions and criticisms of pictures in the exhibitions she visited with her father, accounts of the family holidays in Scotland, of a trip with a friend to the Zoological Gardens and, on July 1882, 'Went to the swimming-baths.' It is liberally sprinkled with jokes and stories, mainly culled from newspapers or related by her father on his return from one of his clubs (he had been elected to the Athenaeum as well as the Reform), and with her comments on the people that she met. It reveals her as a thoughtful, determined and intelligent girl, too often prone to colds and headaches, but with a keen sense of humour and always alert to the issues of the day. She was concerned about the explosions by agitators for Home Rule: 'Friday, March 16th [1883] – What will be blown up next? Last night an attempt was made to blow up the Government Offices in Parliament Street. Not so much damage was done to the building, owing to its great strength, but the streets for some distance round were strewn with glass. One thing struck me as showing the extraordinary power of dynamite, a brick was hurled 100 feet and then through a brick wall into some stables. Someone said the noise was like the 80 ton gun. I believe it was heard here.

'An attempt was also made, but failed, on The Times office, which seems to prove it was the work of Irishmen, that paper having had a leading article in its last number in which it was stated the Irish had got enough and more than enough, and need ask for no more. Papa says it is Mr Gladstone's fault. He takes the side of these rogues and then, if they think he is slackening, they frighten him on a bit – really we shall be as bad as France soon.'

34

From when she was fifteen until she was over thirty, Beatrix kept a journal in a code of her own invention. It was not 'cracked' until 1958. This is Psalm XC (verses 1–9) 'written from memory'.

The problem of Britain's art treasures going out of the country was also of concern. '[*June 1884*] A very celebrated Gallery is to be sold at Christie's soon, Leigh Court, near Bristol; then the rumoured dispersal of the Blenheim pictures proves true. There will be few great collections left in England soon. All the best works of Old Masters leave the Island. The Government is too stingy to buy them, and in the market they are bought cheap for foreign museums, where they of course are settled for life; or for rich Americans, which is much the same as far as their return is concerned.'

In 1882 Rupert Potter photographed the family at Wray Castle, near Windermere, on their first Lake District holiday.

And in the confines of the metropolis Beatrix continued her observations of wild life. '*Saturday, May 19th [1883]* There are such a great many birds this spring. I suppose in consequence of the cold winter. Plenty of blackbirds about here. Pair of hedge sparrows, have only seen these two birds, but have seen the cock-blackbirds fighting, also the cock-robins at the same occupation, but usually only one cock-redbreast, never see a hen. No thrushes about here this spring, not seen tom-tits for a long time. I fancy two wrens about, cock been singing all winter. Two pairs of starlings, one pair from Mrs Crabb's garden, other Mr Beale's. Been very busy getting worms for their young this long time. Seem to begin building beginning of April, use horse dung in their nests.'

The summer holidays of 1882 presented a problem for Rupert Potter. Their beloved Dalguise, virtually the only summer home the children could remember, was no longer available. Its owner, Mr Stuart, had died in Wynberg, Cape Colony, and the house had passed to his heirs – who were raising the rent to an exorbitant

£450. Rupert Potter was forced to look elsewhere. Breaking with tradition, he chose a large house built on the west side of Lake Windermere in the Lake District, Wray Castle. As its name suggests, it was an imposing building, a mock Norman castle, much crenellated. 'This house was built by Mr Dawson, doctor, in 1845, with his wife's money. Her name was Margaret Preston. She was a Liverpool lady. Her father Robert Preston made gin; that was where the money came from. They say it took £60,000 to build it (probably including furniture). It took seven years to finish. The stone was brought across the lake. One old horse dragged it all up to the house on a kind of tram way. The architect, one Mr Lightfoot killed himself with drinking before the house was finished.'

Beatrix was sixteen, and it was her introduction to a part of the country with which she would be associated for ever more.

From mid-July to the end of October the Potters held court at Wray Castle, taking with them the family spaniel, Spot, acquired on one of their Dalguise holidays. The country round about was

(*above left*) While staying at Wray Castle in July 1882, Beatrix painted this water-colour of the library.

(*above right*) Beatrix was devoted to Spot, the family spaniel acquired while on holiday in Scotland.

(*right*) William Gaskell often joined the Potters on their holidays. This group was taken by Rupert Potter at Dalguise in August 1880.

(*below*) A family boating party on Lake Windermere in September 1882. While her father is behind the camera, Beatrix takes the oars.

not unlike Scotland to look at, hills and lakes and tumbling streams. The fishing in the lake was not as good as in the Tay and there were no stags to stalk, but there were tarns to visit and the lake to row on and walks to take. Beatrix and Bertram had new flowers to discover, new plants and animals to draw and new territory to explore. One day they ventured as far as Hawkshead, some two and a half miles away, 'Inquired the way three times, lost continually, alarmed by collies at every farm, stuck in stiles, chased once by cows.'

As before, old friends of the family came to stay, William Gaskell from his church in Manchester and John Bright fresh from his Cabinet resignation over British intervention in Egyptian affairs; Grandmamma Potter travelled up from Camfield full of reminiscences of when the Cromptons owned land in the area. Rupert Potter surrounded himself with those with whom he could discuss politics and religion, painting and literature, and one of the regular visitors to the house was the local vicar, Hardwicke Rawnsley, a good-looking man in his early thirties. Rawnsley was a poet; he had read classics and chemistry at Balliol, had been a keen athlete and oarsman, and was an admirer and friend of John Ruskin, under whose spell he had fallen at Oxford. During his five years as vicar of Wray, the Rev. Rawnsley had grown to love the natural beauty of the Lake District and he was determined that it should be preserved from the incursions of both industry and tourism. He led the fight against the extension of the railway and the plans to close ancient footpaths, he protested at the opening of a new quarry on the fellside and the building of a new coachroad round the lake, and he was preparing to form the Lake District Defence Society, the forerunner of the National Trust. Hardwick Rawnsley had a considerable effect on sixteen-year-old Beatrix. His wife, Edith, painted well and he was interested in Beatrix's obvious artistic talent. He discussed geology and archaeology with her, both subjects about which he was quite knowledgeable, and he introduced her to his conviction of the importance of conservation and protection. Here was someone who loved the things Beatrix loved and who was prepared to fight to preserve them.

In April of the following year, when Bertram Potter was eleven and thought ready for more formal education, he was sent to boarding school in the care of Mr Frederick Hollins at The Grange in Eastbourne. Beatrix's close companion, the brother with whom she had shared so many happy years, was going away. Her governess, Miss Hammond, to whom she had become deeply attached, had reluctantly admitted that her pupil was quickly overtaking her in academic prowess and that she could offer no more. Miss Cameron had left the month before. Once again Beatrix would be alone with her parents in Bolton Gardens. At nearly seventeen, she

A Rupert Potter portrait of Beatrix on 15 October 1882. She was sixteen.

In addition to their summer holidays, the Potters went each April to the seaside. In 1883 they braved the beach at Ilfracombe.

thought that now lessons were over she would be able to concentrate on the one thing that she cared most about, her painting. But Mrs Potter had had other ideas, and on the day before Bertram left for school she appointed a new governess for Beatrix, Miss Anne Carter. Beatrix was not at all pleased. Once again her mother had let her down. 'I thought surely we had got into all the difficulties now, but here is another. A nice way, a lively, to begin with a new governess. If they said I must, I'd do it willingly enough only my temper'd be very nasty – but father wouldn't force me. I thought to have set in view German, English Reading and General Knowledge, cutting off more and more time for painting. I thought to have settled down quietly – but it seems it can not be. Only a year, but if it is like the last it will be a lifetime – I can't settle to anything but my painting, I lost my patience over everything else.'

It was not an auspicious start, but as well as studying German with her new governess, Beatrix continued with her Latin and discovered that it was one of her favourite subjects: '... have finished Dr Arnold, am doing Virgil, like it so much.' Painting lessons were resumed but they took a different turn, with Beatrix going out to an art teacher. 'Am going to Mrs A's for the first time tomorrow, two hours, Monday and Thursday, for twelve lessons. Can have no more because Mrs A's charge is high. Lady Eastlake told papa about her. Of course, I shall paint just as I like when not with her. It will be my first lessons in oil or figure drawing. Of the latter I am supposed to be perfectly ignorant, never having shown my attempts to any one. I may probably owe a good deal to Mrs A as

In June 1883 Beatrix included her pet lizard, Judy, in this water-colour of the pineapple bought for that night's dinner party.

my first teacher. I did to Miss Cameron, but I am convinced it lies chiefly with oneself. Technical difficulties can be taught, and a model will be an immense advantage. We shall see.'

After only her first visit, Beatrix was already having doubts about her teacher. 'Have been to Mrs A's. Am uncertain what to say about it. Believe, though I would not tell any one on any account, that I don't like it, which is rather disappointing. Wish it did not cost so much, is the money being thrown away, will it even do me harm? Don't much like the colours, why should I not use English ones. Linseed oil horrid sticky stuff, she actually used bitumen in her big picture ... I don't mean to say but that she draws and paints pretty well, but I don't like it, it's as smooth as a plate, colour, light and shade, drawing, sentiment.

'It is a risky thing to copy, shall I catch it? I think and hope my self-will which brings me into so many scrapes will guard me here – but it is tiresome, when you do get some lessons, to be taught in a way you dislike and to have to swallow your feelings out of considerations at home and there. Mrs A is very kind and attentive, hardly letting me do anything.' The lessons with Mrs A did not last very long.

As Bertram arrived home for the holidays that summer there was drama in the school room menagerie. 'Toby, one of the lizards we brought from Ilfracombe, departed from this life in the staggers. I think he must have been very old, he was so stiff and had lost so many toes. I think the cause of death was incapacity to derive any benefit from his food. I never saw anything with so little

Edmund Potter died in October 1883, aged eighty-two. Rupert photographed himself with his father at Camfield Place in August of that year.

stomach as he had after he died ... Judy the female lizard laid an egg which unfortunately died in a few hours. It was alive and wriggling with large eyes, tail curled twice, veins and bladder or fluid like a chicken, showing through the transparent brown shell about a quarter inch long, nearly as large as Judy's head.

'The same day Bertram bought for 1/6, at Princes, a pair of hideous little beasties – Sally and Mandar.'

The Potters' dog, Spot, was a constant source of amusement to the children. Spot had a passion for riding in carriages and it was all anyone could do to stop him coming with them when any member of the family set out. One day Cox, the butler, came back with a tale of how he had been taking Spot for a walk in the High Street when a footman threw open the door of a carriage standing at the kerb and Spot jumped straight up into the carriage 'in front of some ladies!'

Annie Carter appeared to tolerate happily all the animal goings-on during the time that she stayed with the Potter family, and she and Beatrix became good friends, though Annie was never other than Miss Carter to her pupil, in spite of there being only three years' difference in their ages.

Towards the end of the summer Grandpapa Potter died. He was in his early eighties and had been ill on and off all year. Although

42

A photograph of Beatrix, aged eighteen, taken by her father at Bush Hall in Hertfordshire in August 1884.

Camfield Place was a large house for an elderly woman to live in alone after more than fifty years of marriage, Grandmamma Potter decided to remain there and the family went to stay more often. She also came to London to stay with her eldest daughter Clara in the old family house in Queen's Gate, and it was there that Beatrix frequently visited her. She was as fond of her grandmother as ever. 'Never saw grandmamma looking better, or livelier, talking about everything, enjoying the jokes, playing whist with her accustomed skill. How pretty she does look with her grey curls, under her muslin cap, trimmed with black lace. Her plain crêpe dress with broad grey linen collar and cuffs turned over. So erect and always on the move, with her gentle face and waken, twinkling eyes. There is no one like grandmamma. She always seems to me as near perfect as is possible here – she looks as if she had as long before her as many of us, but she is eighty-four.'

In June 1885 Annie Carter surprised everyone by announcing that she was leaving to marry a civil engineer called Edwin Moore. Beatrix knew that she would miss her friend and that once again she would be alone, but she also knew that her lessons were at last at an end. 'My education finished 9th July. Whatever moral good and general knowledge I may have got from it, I have retained no literal rules. I don't believe I can repeat a single line of any language. I have liked my last governess best on the whole – Miss Carter had her faults, and was one of the youngest people I have ever seen, but she was very good-tempered and intelligent. I regret German very much, history I can read alone, French is still going on, the rules of geography and grammar are tiresome, there is no general word to express the feelings I have always entertained towards arithmetic.'

Without the restrictions of lessons Beatrix was able to spend more time drawing, but by no means did she stay secluded in the schoolroom. There were other people's pictures to see. She went with her father to the French Gallery at the Tate, where they speculated on the current enthusiasm for Millet and Corot, and then on to see the Turners at the National Gallery, where Beatrix was somewhat taken aback by the swarms of young ladies copying the paintings, 'frightfully for the most part'. She went to charity art exhibitions – 'My father always goes to Exhibitions of that kind because he is curious to see the insides of great houses' – and to the regular shows at 'the greenery yallery' Grosvenor Gallery. As well as looking at pictures, Beatrix accompanied her parents, with somewhat less enthusiasm, to the trade exhibitions at the South Kensington Museum, where she noted afterwards in her journal

Beatrix spent many happy hours in the South Kensington Museum drawing the exhibits. This is the South Court in 1868.

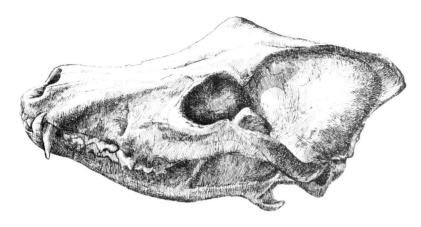

A detailed pen-and-ink study of a wolf's skull, dated by Beatrix 1 January 1886.

what a nuisance babies were to their parents and how unpleasant was the tobacco smoke. She had also learned to drive a carriage, but it was an accomplishment that she restricted to their visits to the country. 'We have a little carriage and pony, the latter aged sixteen is the neatest daisy-cropper I ever saw, and cost £6. It is the first opportunity I have had of learning to drive, like it very much, had no misfortune yet.'

London in 1885 was still suffering the dynamite explosions of Home Rule supporters, and there were frequent and violent demonstrations in the streets by the unemployed, but none of it kept Beatrix in the house.

One day she made up a party for the theatre which took her into quite new territory. 'Went to the Globe with papa and mamma and Edith to see *The Private Secretary*, exceedingly amusing, if one could only have it without the vulgar stammering. I thought the drive there was the most interesting part of the affair. We had to fetch papa from the Athenaeum, but when we got to Buckingham Palace Road her Majesty was having a Drawing-room. We saw the Duchess of Westminster and such grand carriages, and coming home, the Beefeaters marching. We stuck for about half an hour, and after all had to go back round by Westminster, where all the great coaches were drinking at the Inns. Of course papa was in a great state thinking we had had a carriage accident. Extraordinary to state, it was the first time in my life that I had been past the Horse Guards, Admiralty, and Whitehall, or seen the Strand and the Monument.'

When Bertram came home for the holidays it was just like old times. Beatrix bought a tail-less cock-robin from a pet shop for eighteen pence and released it with great satisfaction in the park; they lost a favourite lizard in the garden; and when the time came for Bertram's return to school his sister happily agreed to look after his precious bat. 'It is a charming little creature, quite tame and apparently happy as long as it has sufficient flies and raw meat. I fancy bats are things most people are pleasingly ignorant about.

Beatrix practised her newly acquired skill of driving her pony carriage only in the country. Her father photographed her at Holehird, Windermere, in August 1889.

The Potter children kept animals at home to study and to draw. This bat water-colour by Beatrix was done in January 1885.

Beatrix sent this water-colour of a wood mouse as a Christmas present to a friend in 1886.

I had no idea they were so active on their legs, they are in fact provided with four legs and two wings as well, and their tail is very useful in trapping flies.'

Beatrix, however, soon had to write to Bertram with the news that she was in difficulty. His reply gave her clear instructions about what to do. 'If he cannot be kept alive, as I suppose he can't, you had better kill him, and stuff him as well as you can. Be sure to take his measurements most carefully before you stuff him. That is, the length of head, body, tail, Humerus, Radius, Femoris, Tibia, Pollux and Claw, and also the fingers; in other words all the bones of its wings and legs. I do not know what you had better do to keep the wings stretched out, perhaps if you pinned them out like the bat you got at Edinburgh, but take care if you do so to put some cotton-wool behind its back so that it will not be flat. I should not do to[o] much at its head, as it can't smell much.'

Soon afterwards Beatrix had to cope alone with another sad happening. 'On Oct 18th occurred the death of Poor Miss Mouse, otherwise Xarifa. I was very much distressed, because she had been so sensible about taking medicine that I thought she would get through, but the asthma got over her one night, and she laid herself in my hand and died. Poor little thing, I thought at one time she would last as long as myself.

'I believe she was a great age. Her nose and eyebrows were

white, and towards the end of her life she was quite blind, but affectionate and apparently happy. I wonder if ever another dormouse had so many acquaintances, Mr Bright, Mr J. Millais, and Mr Leigh Smith had admired and stroked her, amongst others. I think she was in many respects the sweetest little animal I ever knew.'*

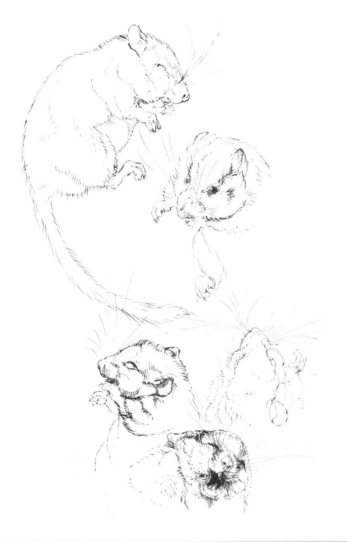

One of Beatrix's favourite pets was a dormouse called Xarifa. These ink-and-pencil studies were made in 1887, the year after Xarifa died.

---

* Over forty years later, when *The Fairy Caravan* was published featuring Xarifa the Dormouse, Beatrix recalled, 'When I was a child I had a favourite dormouse – a sleepy little animal – so we used to say, "Wake up, wake up, Xarifa!" In the real poem it is –

> "Rise up! Rise up! Xarifa!
> Lay the golden cushion down –"

So that was how she got her curious name of Xarifa Dormouse.'

(*right*) Serious illness caused
Beatrix to lose much of her
hair, as can be seen in this
photograph taken by Rupert
Potter at Lingholm, Keswick, in
September 1887. (Only the dog
moved!)

(*below*) Lingholm, Keswick,
today, nearly a hundred years
after the photograph on the
right. Now the home of Lord
Rochdale, the gardens are open
to the public in the summer.

As a child Beatrix had become accustomed to her frequent colds and headaches, but now she was more seriously ill with what was thought to be the start of rheumatic fever. It affected her appearance quite dramatically. 'Had my few remaining locks clipped short at Douglas's. Draughty. My hair nearly all came off since I was ill. Now that the sheep is shorn, I may say without pride that I have seldom seen a more beautiful head of hair than mine. Last summer it was very thick and within about four inches of my knees, being more than a yard long.' Two years later she was even more seriously ill while on an April visit to Grange-over-Sands, with a great deal of pain in her feet and ankles which travelled up to her knees. 'Very little fever, great deal of rheumatics. Could not be turned in bed without screaming out. Continually moving backwards and forwards, up and down each leg, never in more than one place at a time.' When recovered she was amazed to find that she had been ill for so long that the trees had changed from the bareness of winter to the richness of their summer foliage. The illness had affected her heart and it was always to trouble her.

Bertram was also ill that year. He had been taken from his school in Eastbourne and sent to Charterhouse, an institution to which he took a violent dislike. In only his second term there he developed pleurisy, not seriously but enough to frighten his parents into sending him back to Mr Hollins in Eastbourne. The Potters' only flirtation with public schools was short-lived.

For the family summer holidays during the next few years, the Lake District was Rupert Potter's favoured choice, and the house he took most frequently was Lingholm, on the wooded shore of

A sketch made by Beatrix in the summer of 1903 of the view across Derwentwater to St Herbert's Island and Walla Crag behind.

49

(*left*) Benjamin Bouncer, bought in a London bird shop, was the model for Beatrix's first commercial drawing. These pencil sketches were done in 1890.

(*below*) Bertram was also an accomplished artist. He was sixteen when he drew this kestrel.

Derwentwater, near Keswick in Cumberland, where the woods are alive with red squirrels gathering nuts and the lake is perfect for fishing and boating. Winding paths lead down to the lake shore where you look across to St Herbert's Island and Walla Crag rising behind. To the north the stark, heather-clad slopes of Skiddaw tower into the sky, and on the opposite side of the lake, below High Seat, the Lodore Falls thunder down from above. Beatrix had seen nothing like it in Scotland, or even at Wray Castle, and the large-scale grandeur contrasted strongly with her acquaintance with the small, living elements of the Lake District. Her bond with this corner of England, which never diminished when she returned to London, stayed with her all her life.

John Bright often joined the Potters at Lingholm, causing quite a flurry among the local population when he arrived at the station, and entertained the household with up-to-date accounts of the latest political intrigues and with readings of poetry, particularly of Gray's *Elegy* which he read 'very beautifully'.

Beatrix meanwhile had bought a rabbit. 'I brought him home (surreptitiously – if that's the way to spell it) – from a London bird shop in a paper bag. His existence was not observed by the nursery authorities for a week.' She christened the rabbit Benjamin Bouncer and she loved him dearly, taking him with her whenever she went away. He was a marvellous animal to draw.

Beatrix was always drawing, whatever else was happening and wherever she happened to be. One of the greatest admirers of her work was her Uncle Henry, and when he heard that she had set her heart on buying a printing machine but had not enough money for it, he suggested that she might try to earn some by selling her drawings. Had she not, after all, done some beautiful cards for the family that Christmas, cards that any publisher would snap up? With this encouragement Beatrix set about preparing six designs, using Benjamin Bouncer as her model. 'I may mention (better the day better the deed) that my best designs occurred to me in chapel – I was rather impeded by the inquisitiveness of my aunt, and the idiosyncrasies of Benjamin who has an appetite for certain sorts of paint, but the cards were finished by Easter.' They had a list of five publishers to send them to, keeping Raphael Tuck to the last, 'it is such an absurd name to be under obligation to', and when they were disappointingly rejected by the first firm on the list by return of post, Bertram took the drawings by hand to the next firm, Hildesheimer & Faulkner, on his way through London. Mr Faulkner bought them on the spot for £6 and then asked to see more of the artist's work. Beatrix could hardly believe it, and she hugged the news secretly to herself for nearly a week. 'My first act was to give Bounce (what an investment that rabbit has been in spite of the hutches), a cupful of hemp seeds, the consequence being that when

Beatrix was photographed by her father in September 1889, when she was twenty-three.

(*above left*) One of the designs that Beatrix sold to Hildesheimer & Faulkner in 1890 was used as a Christmas card.

(*above right*) Her earliest published illustrations were for Frederic E. Weatherly's *A Happy Pair*, 1890.

I wanted to draw him next morning he was partially intoxicated and wholly unmanageable. Then I retired to bed, and lay awake chuckling till 2 in the morning, and afterwards had an impression that Bunny came to my bedside in a white cotton night cap and tickled me with his whiskers.'

Some of the designs were published as Christmas and New Year cards and others as illustrations, 'by H.B.P.', to a set of verses by Frederic E. Weatherly, in a booklet entitled *A Happy Pair* which sold for 4½d. Helen Beatrix Potter had started her professional career.

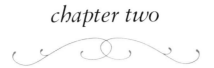

chapter two

'It is something to have a little money
to spend on books and to look forward
to being independent.'

Twenty-five-year-old Beatrix with Benjamin in September 1891

With the confidence that publication gave her, in November 1891 Beatrix submitted some sketches and a booklet to a number of publishers of children's books, among them Frederick Warne. They returned the material to her without a commission: 'We acknowledge the receipt of the sketches and regret that they are of no use to us as we have sometime ago given up publishing Booklets, etc. We are however pleased with the designs and if at any time you have any ideas & drawings in book form, we should be happy to give them our consideration.'

On the rare occasions when her mother was not using the carriage for calling, Beatrix went visiting herself, crossing the river to Baskerville Road in Wandsworth where her old friend, Annie Moore, had moved from Bayswater. Annie's husband, Edwin, was often away working on civil engineering projects abroad, sometimes for more than six months at a time, and Annie was bringing up their young family virtually on her own. There were now four children under four – Noel, so called because he had been born on Christmas Eve, Eric, Marjorie and Winifrede (Freda) who was born in January 1891. Beatrix loved the babies, and often brought her pet mice and rabbits in a basket for them to play with. The warm and friendly atmosphere in Baskerville Road was a welcome contrast to the formality of Bolton Gardens.

For the summer of 1892 the Potters returned to Scotland for the first time in eleven years. They were without their much loved dog, Spot, who had died in April, and they were very conscious of his absence. 'It is the first time for ten years we have travelled without

(*above*) In 1886 Beatrix's governess, Annie Carter, had married Edwin Moore. Beatrix went often to see her quickly-growing family.

(*right*) The Potters took Bedwell Lodge, near Hatfield, for the summer of 1891, before returning to Scotland. Rupert Potter recorded the visit.

him, and coming back to the district where we had him first, I thought it rather pathetic.'

Beatrix was still missing her grandmother, who had died at the age of ninety the previous September, and the whole family were having to face the inevitable sale of their beloved Camfield Place. They were also becoming increasingly worried about Bertram, fearing that he appeared to have inherited his Uncle William

After living alone for eight years, Jessie Potter put Camfield Place on the market and returned to London.

BY ORDER OF THE TRUSTEES OF THE WILL OF THE LATE EDMUND POTTER, ESQ. Deceased.

HERTFORDSHIRE.

In the heart of a most picturesque and exceedingly choice Residential District, about three miles from Hatfield station on the Great Northern Railway (Main Line), six from Hertford, seven from Barnet, eight from St. Albans, and about eighteen from London.

The Particulars, Plan and Conditions of Sale of

THE SINGULARLY ATTRACTIVE

FREEHOLD RESIDENTIAL ESTATE

(PRACTICALLY FREE FROM LAND TAX),

KNOWN AS

"Camfield Place,"

SITUATE IN THE PARISHES OF

HATFIELD & ESSENDON,

AND COMPRISING A

CAPITAL FAMILY MANSION,

With FIRST-RATE STABLING, and all the appurtenances of a COUNTY SEAT.

EXTENSIVE GARDENS AND PLEASURE GROUNDS

Of the most charming description (including large walled KITCHEN GARDENS, Glass Houses, &c.), surrounded by beautifully undulating

Finely Timbered Park Lands of about 150 Acres.

Which, together with the other portions of the Estate, are interspersed with PICTURESQUE WOODLANDS, well watered and affording excellent Preserves for Game.

There are TWO FARM HOUSES (one in two Tenements) with ample FARM BUILDINGS, KEEPER'S LODGE, also several GOOD COTTAGES (mostly modern), and other Premises.

The total area of the Property is about

408a. 0r. 4p.

AND IT INCLUDES PART OF THE MANOR OR REPUTED MANOR OF BEDWELL LOWTHS.

With the exception of certain small portions

POSSESSION WILL BE GIVEN ON COMPLETION OF THE PURCHASE.

FOR SALE BY AUCTION, BY

MESSRS.

DEBENHAM, TEWSON, FARMER & BRIDGEWATER,

At the Mart, Tokenhouse Yard, near the Bank of England,

IN THE CITY OF LONDON,

On TUESDAY, NOVEMBER the 10th, 1891

At TWO o'clock PUNCTUALLY, IN ONE LOT.

May be Viewed by Cards to be had of the Auctioneers. Particulars with Plans and Conditions of Sale may be obtained of Messrs. JANSON, COBB, PEARSON & Co., Solicitors, 41, Finsbury Circus, E.C.; of Messrs. DARBISHIRE, TATHAM & WORTHINGTON, Solicitors, Manchester; of Mr. NOCKOLDS, Land Agent and Surveyor, Saffron Walden, Essex, and 2, Parsons Court, Cambridge; and of

THE AUCTIONEERS, 80, CHEAPSIDE, LONDON, E.C.

Bertram was spending much of his time painting, but his family were becomingly increasingly worried about his drinking.

Leech's fondness for alcohol. Rupert Potter had been called upon more than once in the last few years to rescue Uncle Willie from certain financial difficulties in which he found himself through drink, and Beatrix had been shaken by her uncle's death five years before: 'He had inflammation of the lungs with which he had no chance owing to the horrible condition of his body through drink. The story is so shocking I cannot write it.' Beatrix had been worrying about Bertram for some time: 'The best upbringing has sometimes failed in this family and I am afraid that Bertram has IT in him. Heaven grant it is not so.'

Rupert Potter decided that Oxford might be the answer for his errant son and planned to send him there in October. From the end of July he had rented Heath Park in Birnam for three months, a house only a few miles from Dalguise, and the family travelled up on the overnight train from King's Cross to Perth, laden down with luggage. Beatrix insisted that Benjamin Bouncer was included in the party. 'Benjamin Bunny travelled in a covered basket in the

56

wash-place; took him out of the basket near Dunbar, but proved scared and bit the family.'

Heath Park was a rather smaller house than the Potters were used to, but in Beatrix's eyes this made it almost more acceptable. 'I think myself that a house that is too small is more comfortable than one a great deal too large . . . It is situated at what an auction-eer's clerk would call "a convenient remove" from the Station, mainly up a steep bank and over a hedge. There is a fine view, however, over the top of the Station. The trains prove to be a source of constant amusement. Papa is constantly running out, and looks out of the bedroom window in the night.'

The house did not allow for visitors from London so the Potters settled down happily to their own amusements, under the watchful eye of the gamekeeper Mr McDougall and his wife. Rupert and Bertram fished both the Braan and the Tay, and when 12 August came it was time for the grouse. Rupert spent a great deal of time with his camera and Bertram with his paints, while Beatrix and her mother drove out in the pony cart to visit old friends from the Dal-guise days, including their old cook, Sarah, who had stayed to marry the gamekeeper, and the Dalguise washerwoman, Kitty MacDonald. 'She is a comical, round little old woman, as brown as a berry and wears a multitude of petticoats and a white mutch. Her memory goes back for seventy years and I really believe she is prepared to enumerate the articles of her first wash in the year '71,' the year that she first washed for them at Dalguise. Beatrix also went off alone to sketch and to photograph, for she, too, had dis-covered the pleasure of photography. With a heavy old camera of her father's and with the help of Mr McDougall, 'his keenness for

With a camera inherited from her father, Beatrix discovered the pleasures of photography. Benjamin Bunny was a natural model.

photography is something surprising', Beatrix took pictures of the rabbits that came to raid the garden and of the tame gulls that stole the hens' food next door. She was not always successful and she had a severe critic in McDougall, who 'putting on his spectacles to inspect the result, unkindly said that he couldn't make head or tail o't . . . However he said it was splendid, and said "gosh" in a low tone at appropriate intervals.'

Benjamin had to be cared for, of course, and he was a source of much concern to Beatrix. 'It is not a safe place for Benjamin Bouncer. I walk him about with a leather strap . . . After breakfast taking Mr Benjamin Bunny to pasture at the edge of the cabbage bed with his leather dog-lead, I heard a rustling, and out came a little wild rabbit to talk to him, it crept half across the cabbage bed and then sat up on its hind legs, apparently grunting. I replied, but the stupid Benjamin did nothing but stuff cabbage. The little animal evidently a female, and of a shabby appearance, nibbling, advanced to about three straps length on the other side of my rabbit, its face twitching with excitement and admiration for the beautiful Benjamin, who at length caught sight of it round a cabbage, and immediately bolted. He probably took it for Miss Hutton's cat.' And Benjamin did not only eat cabbage. 'Benjamin's mind has at last comprehended gooseberries, he stands up and picks them off the bush, but has such a comical little mouth, it is a sort of bob cherry business.' And people were constantly giving Benjamin sweets, with dire results; 'Much concerned with the toothache and swollen face of Benjamin Bouncer, whose mouth is so small I cannot see in, but as far as I can feel there is no breakage. This comes of peppermints and comfits. I have been quite indignant with papa and McDougall, though to be sure he is a fascinating little beggar, but unfortunately has not the sense to suck the minties when obtained.'

Even though they were far from London, the Potters kept up with the news from the capital, taking *The Times* as well as the *Scotsman*, and Beatrix recorded in her journal the discussions they had following the death of Lord Tennyson and the appointment of his successor as Poet Laureate, offering her own original solution. 'I hope it will go to a literateur rather than a poetaster. I think Sir Theodore Martin is the likeliest. Another way out of the difficulty would be to give it to Miss Ingelow or Miss Rossetti, which would be comparative peace between two competitors instead of a crowd, and not altogether inappropriate at the end of our good Queen's reign.'

Whenever she went away Beatrix kept up a regular correspondence with her erstwhile governess, Miss Hammond, giving her full accounts of all their adventures and the latest news of their various pets. From Birnam she also wrote to Annie Moore and sent

Rabbits were a favourite subject for Beatrix and she covered pages with sketches of them.

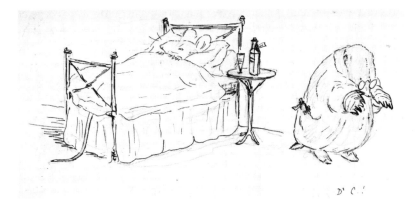

While on holiday at Heath Park in August 1892, Beatrix caricatured Dr Culbard who attended her mother after a fall.

pictures for four-year-old Noel. Throughout the holiday Beatrix continued to draw. She sketched and painted the gently rising hills, the woods of oak, larch and pine and the characteristic weeping birch; she drew animals and birds and flowers, and she caricatured the local doctor who attended her mother after a fall.

Beatrix had two new areas of interest that occupied a great deal of her time, fossils and fungi, and she collected and drew them constantly in minute detail, characteristically becoming extremely

Cantherellula cyathiformis (or little chanterelle) from Dunkeld, painted by Beatrix *c.* 1892.

Charlie McIntosh was the Dunkeld postman and expert on fungi whose opinion Beatrix valued. He found her drawings both pleasing and botanically accurate.

knowledgeable on both subjects. Her fungus drawings brought her into contact again with Charles McIntosh, the postman she remembered from her childhood holidays at Dalguise, an intriguing figure of somewhat startling appearance. 'I would not make fun of him for worlds, but he reminded me so much of a damaged lamp post . . . a more scared startled scarecrow it would be difficult to imagine. Very tall and thin, stooping with a weak chest, one arm swinging and the walking-stick much too short, hanging to the stump with a loop, a long wisp of whisker blowing over either shoulder, a drip from his hat and his nose, watery eyes fixed on the puddles or anywhere, rather than any other traveller's face.'

As the postman for the district, Charlie walked fifteen miles every day making his deliveries, a distance that gave him ample opportunity to study the natural history of the countryside, and over the years he became an expert on the mosses and fungi of the area, being elected an Associate of the Perthshire Society of Natural Science. Beatrix was anxious to get his opinion of her fungus drawings. 'I have been trying all summer to speak with that learned but extremely shy man, it seemed stupid to take home the drawings without having shown them to him . . . He was certainly pleased with my drawings, and his judgement speaking to their accuracy in minute botanical points gave me infinitely more pleasure than that of critics who assume more, and know less than poor Charlie. He is a perfect dragon of erudition, and not gardener's Latin either.' Beatrix had confirmation that the work she had set herself was good. Scotland had once again worked its magic spell.

In the middle of October Bertram duly departed for Oxford, 'with the Jay crammed into a little box, kicking and swearing. Mamma expressed her uncharitable hope that we might have seen the last of it . . . It is an entertaining, handsome bird, but unsuitable for the house.' Predictably, sending Bertram to Oxford did not solve anything and it was not long before both he and the jay were home again.

For the next two summers the Potters returned north of the border for their holidays, in 1893 to Eastwood, a dower house on the Atholl Estate beside the river Tay in Dunkeld, and the following year to Lennel in Coldstream, a house with 'a splendid view over the valley to the Cheviot Hills'. It was from Eastwood, on 4 September 1893, that Beatrix wrote the picture letter to Noel Moore that was to become one of the most famous letters ever written. 'My dear Noel, I don't know what to write to you, so I shall tell you a story about four little rabbits whose names were Flopsy, Mopsy, Cottontail and Peter . . .'

Beatrix had bought a Belgian rabbit from London 'in the Uxbridge Road, Shepherds Bush, for the exorbitant sum of 4/6'.

Eastwood Dunkeld
Sep 4ᵗ 93

My dear Noel,
I don't know what to write to you, so I shall tell you a story about four little rabbits whose names were—

Flopsy, Mopsy Cottontail

and Peter

They lived with their mother in a sand bank under the root of a big fir tree.

She had christened him Peter Piper and taught him to do tricks for the amusement of visiting children. Like his predecessor, Benjamin, Peter went everywhere with her. She drew him from every conceivable angle and she was utterly devoted to him. When he died nine years later Beatrix wrote, 'whatever the limitations of his intellect or outward shortcomings of his fur, and his ears and toes, his disposition was uniformly amiable and his temper unfailingly sweet. An affectionate companion and a quiet friend.'

(*above*) From Eastwood, Dunkeld, on 4 September 1893, Beatrix sent this picture letter to Noel Moore about a rabbit called Peter.

This was also the time when Beatrix was drawing guinea-pigs. Through buying her hats from the same milliner in Sloane Square as the ladies who lived round the corner in Bolton Gardens, Beatrix had discovered to her surprise and delight that there were guinea-pigs at No. 28. The hats were always delivered to Bolton Gardens by two young children of the milliner, Ivy and Jack Hunt, whose mother was a friend of the lady's maid at No. 28, whom they called 'Aunt Jessie'. One day the children were caught in a shower with only a paper bag to protect their precious burden, and when they arrived at the Potters' house they were in some trepidation, fearing that the hats might have been ruined. Instead of the expected reprimand they were taken inside and given dry clothes and cakes and tea, and in the course of this unexpected treat they talked a lot about the guinea-pigs of whom they were very fond. Beatrix became a close friend of the Pagets at No. 28 and was often invited to their lunch parties. Elizabeth Ann Paget (Nina) sometimes lent Beatrix the odd guinea-pig or two to draw, a generous

Beatrix's drawings of her neighbour's guinea-pigs were to be published nearly thirty years later in *Cecily Parsley's Nursery Rhymes*.

gesture which was not always entirely without risk. 'Miss Paget has an infinite number of guinea-pigs. First I borrowed and drew *Mr Chopps*. I returned him safely. Then in an evil hour I borrowed a very particular guinea-pig with a long white ruff, known as *Queen Elizabeth*. This PIG – offspring of *Titwillow the Second*, descendant of the *Sultan of Zanzibar*, and distantly related to a still more illustrious animal named the *Light of Asia* – this wretched pig took to eating blotting paper, pasteboard, string and other curious substances, and expired in the night. I suggested something was wrong and intended to take it back. My feelings may be imagined when I found it extended a damp – very damp disagreeable body. Miss Paget proved peaceable, I gave her the drawing.'

The next few years were important ones for Beatrix and her horizons were quickly widening. Shortly before her twenty-eighth birthday, she was invited to stay with her distant cousin, Caroline Hutton, who lived at Harescombe Grange near Stroud in Gloucester. 'I went to Harescombe on Tuesday the 12th of June. I used to

(*above*) The Potters' 1894 spring holiday was in Falmouth, where Beatrix was duly photographed by her father on 31 March.

(*left*) For the summer of 1894 the family took Lennel House, near Coldstream, and from there they went on numerous expeditions into the Border Country.

(*above*) Caroline Hutton, Beatrix's cousin, whom she visited in Gloucestershire in June 1894. It was the first time she had been away alone for five years.

(*right*) Beatrix tricked Caroline's father, Crompton Hutton, to sit for a photograph by asking him to check a quotation from Milton for her.

go to my grandmother's, and once I went for a week to Manchester, but I had not been away independently for five years. It was an event.' The visit was a great success. Beatrix took to Mrs Hutton on sight, and to Caroline's father, Crompton Hutton, when she got used to him; she liked her cousins, particularly Caroline, and in following years Beatrix returned to Gloucestershire many times.

She also made her first visit to her Uncle Fred Burton, married to another of the Leech sisters, Harriet, who had moved from Manchester to a large old house, Gwaynynog, in the rich, undulating countryside near Denbigh. Fred Burton had bought Gwaynynog in a dilapidated state from the Myddleton family, whose ancestral home it was but who had dissipated whatever money they might have had and been reduced to living in the kitchen. Uncle Fred did

PLATE VII (above) The view from 2 Bolton Gardens at dusk in November.

PLATE VIII (right) Some of Miss Paget's many guinea pigs, borrowed by Beatrix in 1893.

PLATE IX (left) Beatrix loved flowers and collected and painted them wherever she went.

PLATE X (below) *Leccinum scabrum*, found by Beatrix while on holiday at Lingholm, near Keswick, in October 1897.

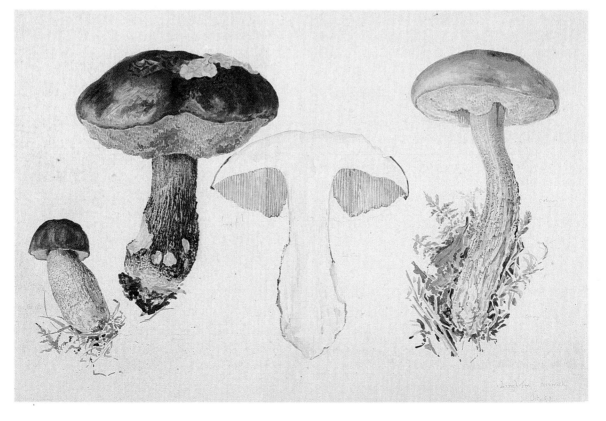

not stint on redecoration or on furnishing. Like a good Lancashire man he had made his fortune in cotton and instructed that the cotton plant should be used as an emblem in the house wherever possible, and it can be seen there today, incorporated into the decoration of the fenders round the fires and in the carving on the old furniture. Beatrix was intrigued by Wales – and terrified by her uncle's driving, 'sublimely unconscious of the fact that he cannot drive'. She thought her cousin, Alice, 'rather quiet'.

Beatrix kept up her regular visits to the Moores in Wandsworth where there were now five children, Norah (Bardie) joining her two brothers and two sisters. She also went as far as Maidenhead to see Miss Hammond 'in a little red-tiled cottage on the common at Pinkney Green', but she found the journey uncomfortable and expensive 'so I am afraid Miss Hammond will see few visitors'.

Beatrix's interests and enthusiasms at this time were wide-ranging, and on a number of subjects she was remarkably well-informed, considering that she was almost entirely self-taught. Her fossil collection was growing fast as she searched quarries and crumbling walls in Scotland and the Lake District, split stones with a cold chisel in Gloucestershire, and took her treasures home to draw and to identify at the Natural History Museum. She photographed whenever the opportunity arose and had a precious new camera with a 'lovely mahogany complexion'. With her cousin

Gwaynynog, near Denbigh, in 1895, the year that Beatrix went to stay with her Uncle Fred Burton for the first time.

In 1892 Beatrix meticulously recorded some of the finds from an archaeological dig of twenty years before in the City of London.

Alice she took lessons in Platinotype printing, and she was learning all of Shakespeare's plays by heart: 'I learnt six more or less in a year. Never felt the least strained or should not have done it.' She made intricate studies and detailed watercolours of insects, finding the 'Index' collection at the Museum 'an extreme example of museum labelling run mad'. From a friend she borrowed a number of Roman remains and relics that had been found twenty years before on a site in the City of London, and recorded them in a series of water-colours and drawings.

It was at this time, too, that Beatrix offered to a firm of fine art colour printers, Ernest Nister, for whom she had been doing a considerable number of small commissions, an illustrated story from one of her letters to Noel Moore about a frog called Mr Jeremy Fisher. She thought that perhaps it might be made into a booklet. Nisters were not attracted by the idea – 'We certainly cannot make a booklet of it as people do not want frogs now' – but they bought the drawings and put them into one of their children's annuals.

Although Ernest Nister rejected Beatrix's idea for a story about a frog, they bought some of her drawings for their children's annuals.

The earning of her own money was a source of great comfort to Beatrix at a time when her father was becoming ill and difficult and her mother was as demanding as ever. 'It is something to have a little money to spend on books and to look forward to being independent, though forlorn.' She was approaching her thirtieth birthday, and though her health had never been good, it seemed that as she gained in age so she gained in strength. 'I feel much younger at thirty than I did at twenty; firmer and stronger both in mind and body.'

Beatrix's strength of will was clearly tested later that year when she came up against the specialists at the Royal Botanic Gardens at Kew. Her interest in lichen and fungi, which had begun in Scotland and been nurtured and encouraged there by the self-effacing Charlie McIntosh, had become a subject of considerable importance to her. She studied spores under her microscope and even

The Potters stayed at Lakefield (now Ees Wyke), Sawrey, in the summer of 1896, and Rupert Potter photographed his daughter in Hawkshead on 10 August, outside the Courthouse (called 'The Grange' by him).

tried cultivating new spores, and she recorded in her journal her fascination with the Pasteurs' experiments with penicillium as she drew and painted specimen after specimen. Her drawings much impressed her uncle, Sir Henry Roscoe, and he introduced Beatrix to his friend, Mr Thiselton-Dyer, the director of Kew Gardens, with a request for a ticket to visit and study there. There was no trouble about the ticket – 'He seemed pleased with my drawings and a little surprised' – and Beatrix went to Kew frequently during the ensuing months, fascinated by the work with fungi being done there. The trouble started when she was convinced that she had discovered a way to grow spores and was anxious to know if she was right. Her reception at Kew was cool, particularly by Mr George Massee, a principal assistant there, and her work was virtually dismissed, though Beatrix felt that she detected an underlying interest and reflected that one day she might see her theories appearing in someone else's book without acknowledgement. So she persisted, and detailed her research in a paper, 'On the Germination of the Spores of *Agaricineae*, by Miss Helen B. Potter', which was read to the Linnean Society of London on 1 April 1897. It was not read by Beatrix, as ladies were not allowed to attend the society's meetings, but by Mr George Massee, F.L.S., the same man who had given her such a cool reception at Kew.

Beatrix and her family now holidayed in the Lake District every summer, usually staying at Lingholm near Keswick. Hardwicke Rawnsley, the vicar of Wray when the Potters first went to Wray Castle, remained a close friend, particularly to Beatrix. He had moved from Wray to be vicar of Crosthwaite, just the other side of Keswick from Lingholm, and with his wife had set up a

Beatrix's work on the germination of spores was finally recognized when her paper was presented to the Linnean Society in London in 1897.

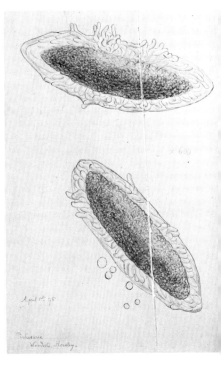

school of industrial arts in an effort to preserve the hand-crafting of goods and to combat the cheap imports that were flooding the country from Germany and Japan. Hardwicke Rawnsley was a busy man; as well as running his parish and his school he was Honorary Canon of Carlisle, the Honorary Secretary of the newly-formed National Trust for Places of Historic Interest and Natural Beauty, and was regularly publishing sonnets, appreciations of Lakeland poets and guides to the Lake District. He had also written an extraordinary collection of verses for children, *Moral Rhymes for the Young*, which was turning out to be widely popular. It was not altogether surprising, therefore, that Beatrix turned

(*opposite*) Wherever she was staying Beatrix drew and painted. This water-colour of cocks' heads was done in August 1899.

Beatrix greatly admired Hardwicke Rawnsley, and her father photographed them, together with young Noel Rawnsley, in the garden at Lingholm.

a great many carriages, one fat old gentleman always amuses me, he has the very smallest grey ponies in little blue & red coats.

My pony must be having a lazy time, I shall come and see you some day when it is fine.

yrs. aff - Beatrix Potter -

The Moore children treasured their letters from Beatrix. This one to Marjorie Moore was sent from Hastings on 13 January 1899.

to her friend Canon Rawnsley for advice when, in 1900, she had an idea that she might find a publisher for a children's book she had written.

The Tale of Peter Rabbit and Mr McGregor's Garden 'by H.B. Potter' was based on the picture letter Beatrix had written to Noel Moore from Dunkeld seven years before. The Moore children prized their letters from Beatrix highly and always kept them safely, Marjorie carefully tying hers into a bundle with yellow ribbon. When Beatrix came to copy out Noel's story about Peter Rabbit she decided that it needed to be longer to make a book, and she added a whole middle section of Peter's adventures while trying to find his way out of Mr McGregor's garden. His meeting with the mouse with the pea in his mouth and his seeing the white cat were put in at this stage, as was Peter's exhausted sleep when he arrived home. She substituted a sieve for Mr McGregor's

The four older Moore girls, Marjorie, Winifred, Norah (seated on chair) and Joan, were photographed in 1900, probably by Rupert Potter.

basket, and brought in the sparrows to urge Peter to free himself from the gooseberry net.

Beatrix prepared her new manuscript in a lined exercise book, each page with a black-and-white pen-and-ink drawing facing the text and with a coloured illustration as a frontispiece. Beatrix and Canon Rawnsley sent it off in great expectation but as the manuscript came back without an offer from at least six publishers in turn, Beatrix began to lose hope. One publisher did show some interest but he wanted to change Beatrix's proposed size of the book, something to which she would not agree: 'The publisher is a gentleman who prints books, and he wants a bigger book than he has got enough money to pay for! and Miss Potter has arguments with him ... I think Miss Potter will go off to another publisher soon! She would rather make two or three little books costing 1/- each, than one big book costing 6/- because she thinks little rabbits

"Your Father had an accident there; he was put in a pie by Mrs McGregor "

A spread from the manuscript for the privately printed *Peter Rabbit*. Mrs McGregor was redrawn in colour as a younger woman for the first Warne edition, and the picture was dropped altogether for the fifth printing.

cannot afford to spend six shillings on one book.' So Beatrix took matters into her own hands. She would pay to have the book printed and she would publish it herself.

For advice about a printer Beatrix went to a friend in the Natural History Museum, a Miss Woodward, 'who knew something about engraving and printing'. Gertrude was the sister of Alice B. Woodward who had illustrated a number of children's books and was, some six years later, to provide the full colour plates for the first narrative edition of *Peter Pan*. There were seven Woodward children, the three eldest daughters all artists, and as their father, Dr Henry Woodward, was Keeper of Geology at the British Museum and editor of *The Geographical Magazine*, Gertrude was in a good position to advise Beatrix. She recommended a London printer called Strangeways & Sons and Beatrix went ahead, ordering 250 copies of what she now called *The Tale of Peter Rabbit*. The book was ready on 16 December 1901 and made an excellent Christmas present for Beatrix's friends and relations. The copies that she did not give away she sold for 1/2d each. The little book was an immediate success, with Beatrix receiving letters of appreciation and news of its reception from various directions; 'Conan Doyle had a copy for his children and he has a good opinion of the story and words.' Within a week or two copies were running out and, in order not to disappoint her customers, Beatrix had a further 200 copies printed.

An old mouse was running in and out over the stone door-step, carrying peas and beans to her family in the wood. Peter asked her the way to the gate? but she had such a large pea in her mouth that she could not answer. She shook her head at him. Peter began to cry again.

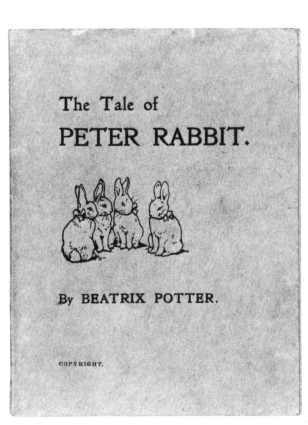

The Tale of
PETER RABBIT.

By BEATRIX POTTER.

COPYRIGHT.

(*above*) Frederick Warne decided to publish *Peter Rabbit* on condition that Beatrix would redo the pictures in colour. She took the opportunity to make some changes to the text.

(*left*) The cover of the privately printed *The Tale of Peter Rabbit*, which was issued by Beatrix on 16 December 1901.

Meanwhile Canon Rawnsley had not given up in his efforts to find a commercial publisher for *Peter Rabbit*, even going to the trouble of rewriting Beatrix's text in verse, beginning with:

> There were four little bunnies
> – no bunnies were sweeter
> Mopsy and Cotton-tail,
> Flopsy and Peter.

Continuing until:

> They sat down to tea
> Too good mannered to cram
> and ate bread and milk
> and sweet blackberry jam.

One of the publishers he sent it to was Frederick Warne, the company which had ten years before seen Beatrix's drawings and asked to consider 'any idea and drawings in book form' she might have. The partners of Warne were divided in their views about what they called 'the bunny book' and they sought the advice of one of their most successful artists, Leslie Brooke, whose recent illustrations for Edward Lear's *The Pelican Chorus* and *The Jumblies* had received a great deal of praise. Acting on Leslie Brooke's advice that they should go ahead and publish 'as it would undoubtedly be a success', Warne wrote to Canon Rawnsley to say that they might take the book but they did not much like the verses. 'We think there is a great deal to be said for simple narration which has been very effectively used in a little book produced last year entitled *Little Black Sambo*.' They also insisted that the illustrations should be in colour, to which Beatrix when she was informed replied, 'I did not colour the book for two reasons – the great expense of colour printing – and also the rather uninteresting colour of a good many of the subjects which are most of them rabbit-brown and green.' However, Warne persisted, and before Beatrix's own privately printed edition of the book was published, they had persuaded her to agree to redo the illustrations in colour.

In order to keep their published price of the book down to 1/6d, they offered her a penny a copy on the first edition, the grand sum of £20 in all. Beatrix thought their terms 'very liberal', indeed she was even prepared to forgo her penny if it would mean a published price of more than 1/6d, and she agreed that they should go ahead, even though she was slightly apprehensive of her father's reaction. 'I have not spoken to Mr Potter, but I think Sir, it would be well to explain the agreement clearly, because he is a little formal having been a barrister.' Canon Rawnsley's verses were abandoned and Beatrix carefully revised her text before she started work on the

This picture by Bertram shows that he was more competent than his sister at drawing figures. By 1902 Bertram was a full-time artist.

new colour illustrations. She was still working on them while in Scotland on holiday with Bertram in May of 1902: 'My brother is sarcastic about the figures; what you and he take for Mr McGregor's nose was intended for his ear, not his nose at all . . . I never learnt to draw figures.'

Bertram was becoming a problem. Since his unhappy, and very brief, time at Oxford he had spent most of his time painting – and drinking. To escape from the restrictions of home life he went on frequent sketching trips to the north of England and to Scotland, always accompanied by a man 'to carry his easel' but really to

'Then old Mrs Rabbit took a basket'. One of the preliminary sketches for *The Tale of Peter Rabbit.*

(*below right*) 'And squeezed under the gate!' The black-and-white line drawing from the privately printed *Peter Rabbit.* The spread is now in colour and carries more text.

restrain his drinking. It was on one of these trips to Birnam some years later that he fell in love with Mary Scott, a girl from Hawick in Scotland who was helping in the house where he was staying. Bertram was to marry Mary secretly and become a farmer, leaving behind once and for all the disapproving attentions of his parents, though seven years were to pass before they discovered that he was not farming alone up in Ancrum on the Borders.

Plans for the publication of *Peter Rabbit* were proceeding well. The publishers decided to issue two editions, one bound in cloth to be sold for 1/6d and the other in paper boards for 1/-, a decision welcomed by Beatrix who wanted the book to be as cheap as possible. She had delayed visiting the Warne office to sign the contract: 'I could not well leave Mrs Potter. She is getting better now, but I am sadly afraid will be deaf; the drum of one ear being broken and the other very bad. It was influenza.' Beatrix thought she would come and see the first proofs of the colour illustrations, although she added a cautionary note to her letter: 'If my father happens to insist on going with me to see the agreement, would you please not mind him very much, if he is fidgetty about things. I am afraid it is not a very respectful way of talking and I don't wish to refer to it again, but I think it is better to mention beforehand he is sometimes a little difficult; I can of course do what I like about the book being 36. I suppose it is a habit of old gentlemen; but sometimes rather trying.'

The contract, signed at last in June 1902, gave no payment at all to the author on the first 3,000 copies of the 1/- edition but a 10 per cent royalty on the 1/6d edition, 'thirteen copies to be reckoned as twelve', a 'baker's dozen', and normal practice. Beatrix took a very close interest in every aspect of the production, commenting knowledgeably on the proofs of the illustrations and how the colours might be adjusted, and she was making final changes to the text until the very last moment. The Frederick Warne edition of *The Tale of Peter Rabbit* was published on 2 October 1902 and orders had been received for the entire first printing of 8,000 copies beforehand.

chapter three

'He did not live long, but he fulfilled
a useful happy life.'

Norman Warne and Beatrix Potter

THROUGHOUT 1901 and 1902 Beatrix had been exchanging letters with her publisher, and she was now a regular visitor to the office in Bedford Street, Covent Garden, the carriage waiting outside to whisk her back to Bolton Gardens the minute business was completed. Three months before *Peter Rabbit* was published there was already talk of a new book, Beatrix sending some colour drawings and suggesting that she use them to illustrate a number of rhymes, starting with one about Cecily Parsley, a book in the style of 'Caldecott's and *The Baby's Opera*'.

In the office in Bedford Street was a young man, Norman Warne, a son of the founder of the company, Frederick Warne. Norman's two older brothers, Harold and Fruing, were also in the business, both of them married and with children of their own, but it was Norman with whom Beatrix always corresponded. He lived in the imposing family house at No. 8 Bedford Square with his mother, a widow since Frederick Warne's death in 1901, and with

Beatrix's publisher, Frederick Warne, with his wife Louisa and two of their six children, Millie and Fruing.

(*above*) When Fruing Warne married Mary Stephens on 27 April 1898, his youngest brother Norman (third from the right) was best man.

(*left*) After her husband's death in 1901, Louisa Warne lived at 8 Bedford Square with her unmarried children, Millie and Norman.

his unmarried sister, Amelia (Millie), a meek and indecisive girl who Norman affectionately called 'Old Mill', quite unlike the other members of the family to look at, owing it was said in the family 'to the fact that she was a Crimean baby'. Norman's eldest brother, Frederick, had died when quite young and his other sister, Edith, had moved away on her marriage. Norman was the baby, his mother's 'ugly duckling', though he was an attractive fellow, tall and dark; some said he was not unlike Robert Louis Stevenson to look at. He was undoubtedly his mother's favourite and warmly cared for by her and by his sister. Between Norman and Beatrix there was a strong friendship growing up. Though it was always 'Mr Warne' and 'Miss Potter', that was an advance on the 'Sir' and 'Madam' with which they had begun their correspondence and their letters were becoming more and more relaxed.

Meanwhile Beatrix was preparing to publish a second book privately. On one of her visits to her cousin, Caroline, in Gloucestershire, she had heard the strange tale of how a tailor in the City of Gloucester had left in his workshop one Saturday a waistcoat, cut out but not made up. When he returned on the following Monday, the waistcoat was finished, all but one buttonhole, to which was fastened a scrap of paper with the message 'No more twist'. Beatrix was intrigued by the tale and she had used it as the basis for a long story, written out in an exercise book and with twelve colour illustrations, which she had given the year before as a Christmas present to Freda Moore. The success of the privately printed *Peter Rabbit* prompted Beatrix to think that *The Tailor of Gloucester* might make a good follow-up, and as Warne had not yet published their *Peter Rabbit* and would be hardly likely to want a second book so soon, Beatrix went ahead on her own. She printed 500 copies and published in October 1902, sending a copy to Norman Warne on 17 December: 'I hope that at all events you will not think the story very silly.' Norman was delighted with it and suggested at once that Warne might publish it but in a shortened version, a suggestion that caused Beatrix some amusement. 'Thank you for your letter about the mouse book. You have paid it the compliment of taking the plot very seriously; and I perceive that your criticisms are just; because I was quite sure in advance that you would cut out the tailor and all my favourite rhymes! Which was one of the reasons why I printed it myself.'

Norman Warne was now in something of a dilemma, as ideas were following one after another from his new author. As well as the book of rhymes and *The Tailor of Gloucester*, there was a proposal for a book about some squirrels. This came in a letter from Beatrix while she was staying with her cousin, Ethel, Lady Hyde Parker, in the family's beautiful house, Melford Hall in Suffolk. 'I only hope the gamekeeper will succeed in getting a squirrel before I

PLATE XI The garden at Lakefield in Sawrey, where Beatrix was staying in 1896 · when she first discovered Hill Top Farm.

PLATE XII (right) An 1890s
Christmas-card design for
Hildesheimer & Faulkner,
redrawn in 1917 as the
frontispiece for *Appley Dapply*.

PLATE XIII (below) Inscribed:
'Aug.99 Peter Rabbit – he had
an old quilt made of scraps of
flanel and blue cloth which he
always lay on.'

leave on Monday,' she wrote, because she badly needed one as a model. Then the matter of the frog book came up again: 'I should like to do Mr Jeremy Fisher too some day.' After consultation within Frederick Warne, the decision was made to do two books, *The Tailor of Gloucester* and the squirrel story, *The Tale of Squirrel Nutkin*, and to publish them both in time for Christmas 1903. 'I think my sympathies are still with the poor old tailor,' wrote Beatrix, 'but I can well believe the other would be more likely to appeal to people who are accustomed to a more cheerful Christmas than I am.'

Christmas was often a sad time of year for her. As a child she had been particularly vulnerable to the cold and the London fog and many a Christmas had been spent alone and in bed. Grandmother Leech had been dying at Christmas in 1883, and in 1895 Beatrix noted in her journal, 'We had not a pleasant Christmas, wet, dark, Bertram sulky ... By the middle of the week Papa was ill, very ill he looked last night.' The Potters' Unitarian allegiance

Melford Hall in Suffolk, where Beatrix was planning a squirrel book when she stayed with her cousin, Ethel, in 1902.

81

I believe that his name was Nutkin and that he had a brother called Twinkleberry, and this is the story of how he lost his tail —

There is a big island in the middle of the lake, covered with woods, and in the middle of it stands a hollow oak-tree which is the house of an owl, called Old Brown. One autumn when the nuts were ripe, Nutkin and Twinkleberry, and all the other

The Tale of Squirrel Nutkin
was first told in this picture
letter to Norah Moore,
written from Lingholm on
25 September 1901.

kept them from participating in the usual Christian festivals and Beatrix sometimes felt left out. Christmas at No. 2 Bolton Gardens had always been a sober affair in comparison with the celebrations of the Pagets at No. 28 – 'How pretty Miss Paget's tree used to be with the little doll angel up on the top' – and Beatrix knew full well that the Christmas of 1902 would be no different, particularly with Bertram no longer at home.

The new year soon came, however, and Beatrix was really getting into her stride with her books. It seemed as if she was being swept along on a tidal wave of creativity and, moreover, carrying her publisher along with her. Terms for the two new books were agreed and the contracts were signed while she was staying at Gwaynynog in February. 'I am quite satisfied with the agreements; my cotton-spinning uncle thinks the percentage very good; and I think the same.' Like *Peter Rabbit*, *The Tale of Squirrel Nutkin* had first been told in one of Beatrix's picture letters, this one to Norah Moore. It had been sent to her in 1901 while Beatrix was on holiday at Lingholm in the Lake District. As before, the letter was borrowed back from the child and then used as a basis for a much revised version for the book. For the drawings Beatrix was hampered by not having a model for Nutkin and his cousins, and as the gamekeeper had failed to get her a squirrel, Beatrix resorted to the pet shop. 'I bought two but they weren't a pair, and fought so frightfully that I had to get rid of the handsomer – and most savage one – The other squirrel is rather a nice little animal, but half of one ear has been bitten off, which spoils his appearance!' Her other problem was drawing Old Mr Brown, the owl who guarded the nuts on Owl Island. 'I thought my owls very bad when I went again to the [Zoological] Gardens.' However, help was at hand. 'I am going to meet my brother at the Lakes tomorrow; I think he could very likely improve that owl.'

Early sketches of Old Brown, the owl in *Squirrel Nutkin*, which was published for Christmas 1903.

Simultaneously, Beatrix was working on the shortened version of *The Tailor of Gloucester*. She discovered a perfect model for the cherry-coloured coat: 'I have been delighted to find I may draw some most beautiful 18th century clothing at S. Kensington museum, I have been looking at them for a long time in an inconvenient dark corner of the goldsmith's court, but had no idea they could be taken out of the case. The clerk says I could have any article put on a table in one of the offices; which will be most convenient.' She drew the fireplace at Melford Hall for the tailor's kitchen, and she bought some mice while on holiday with her parents in Folkestone.

Beatrix again watched carefully over the production of both books, discussing with Norman Warne not only the paper to be used and the way the pictures should be printed but going into considerable detail about the endpapers and the binding: 'I always think that an end paper ought to be something to rest the eye between the cover and the contents of the book; like a plain mount for a framed drawing.' As with *Peter Rabbit*, both books were to be issued in two bindings, one in paper and the de-luxe edition in cloth, and it was with the cloth binding that Beatrix was able to help, sending for calico samples from the family firm in Manchester: 'If they had any *pattern* suitable there would of course be no

(*opposite*) Beatrix shortened her privately printed *The Tailor of Gloucester* for the Warne edition. This pencil sketch for a painting book was finally never used.

The de luxe editions of *The Tailor of Gloucester* and *Squirrel Nutkin*, published by Warne in 1903, were bound in patterned calico supplied by Edmund Potter and Company.

came again to Bedford St.; it seemed a pity to have different opinions about it, after having agreed so pleasantly about the rabbit book. I think it will work out all right. I remain yrs sincerely Beatrix Potter.

N D Warne Esq
15 Bedford St.

reduced
by
$\frac{1}{3}$

by $\frac{1}{4}$

(*above*) At the end of a letter to Norman Warne of 5 February 1903, Beatrix sketched her suggestion for the cover picture of *Squirrel Nutkin*.

(*right*) A rough sketch by Beatrix of the squirrels making their offering of three fat mice to Old Brown, from the manuscript of *Squirrel Nutkin*.

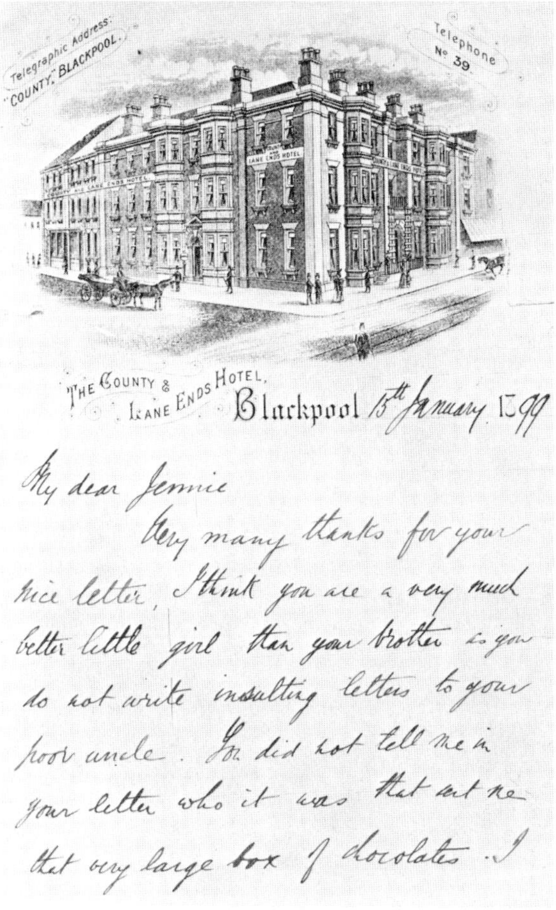

The letterhead reads: Telegraphic Address: "COUNTY, BLACKPOOL." — Telephone No 39 — THE COUNTY & LANE ENDS HOTEL. Blackpool 15th January 1899

My dear Jennie

Very many thanks for your nice letter, I think you are a very much better little girl than your brother as you do not write insulting letters to your poor uncle. You did not tell me in your letter who it was that sent me that very large box of chocolates. I

Norman Warne wrote regularly to his nieces and nephews whenever he went to sell books away from London.

difficulty in getting E. Potter & Co to print in any desired shade of colour, or cloth.' At last all the details were resolved, and *The Tale of Squirrel Nutkin* was scheduled for publication in August 1903 and the new version of *The Tailor of Gloucester* for October.

When the books were finished Beatrix felt quite lost. The year had been a hectic one, full of work, much of it done 'on the wing' in Wales, Suffolk, Kent and Gloucestershire. Now there stretched before her the long summer in the Lake District alone with her parents, far from the excitements of her publishers' office and the assiduous attention of her editor, Norman. It would be nice, she thought, if she had some work to do to pass the time. 'I had been a little hoping too that something might be said about another book, but I did not know that I was the right person to make the suggestion! I could send you a list to consider, there are plenty in a vague state of existence, and one written out in a small copybook which I will get back from the children and send to you to read.' Norman was away when Beatrix's letter arrived, for as well as looking after the editing of certain authors' books, part of his duties was to go on extended selling trips, visiting booksellers round the country to show them the new books and to solicit orders for them. Beatrix's letter was answered by his eldest brother, Harold, and he invited Beatrix to come and talk to him about what she would like to do next. This was not at all what Beatrix had intended. 'I regret that I cannot call again at the offices before leaving town. If I had not supposed that the matter would be dealt with through the post, I should not have mentioned the subject of another book at present. I have had such painful unpleasantness at home this winter about the work that I should like a rest.' It was Norman that she wanted to see. 'If you do not forward Mr Norman Warne's letters, will you please tell him sometime I was much obliged for his of July 4th, as he might think I did not acknowledge it.'

Harold Warne tried again, sending Beatrix her finished copies of *Squirrel Nutkin* before she left for the Lakes and encouraging her to send rough outlines of her proposed stories so that they could consider them while she was away. In spite of Norman's absence, she agreed, adding, 'I think I will send the rabbit story as well when I have copied it out, perhaps Mr Norman Warne might be amused to look over it when he comes back.' When shortly afterwards the proofs of *The Tailor of Gloucester* colour illustrations followed Beatrix to Fawe Park, near Keswick, she was much distressed to discover that the printers had cut away the black line she had carefully put round each drawing. 'I think that one of the gateway is intirely spoilt by it. I relied on the line, to make the snow in the foreground look white ... I asked particularly last winter if the line would be left ... The black frame pulls them

Fawe Park, Derwentwater, in 1984. In the summer of 1903 the Potters took the house, near Keswick, for their annual holiday.

At Fawe Park Beatrix was working on an idea for a book about Peter Rabbit's cousin, Benjamin.

together and sends back the distance.' Beatrix was already a very important author on the Warne list, and by the time Norman returned at the end of August the lines had been restored. Norman brought with him good news of the reception for *Squirrel Nutkin*, and Beatrix was happy to be in touch with him again. 'I am *delighted* to hear such a good account of Nutkin, I never thought when I was drawing it that it would be such a success – though I think you always had a good opinion of it. I should be glad to have a few more copies when convenient; it must be a troublesome business to distribute 10,000.'

Norman also responded with enthusiasm to the idea for 'the rabbit story', and Beatrix was occupying her time at Fawe Park well. 'I think I have done every imaginable rabbit background, and miscellaneous sketches as well – about 70! I hope you will like them, though rather scribbled. I had a funny instance of rabbit ferocity last night; I had been playing with the ferret, and then with the rabbit without washing my hands. She, the rabbit, is

Norman Warne often took his nephew, Fred, to play tennis at his brother Fruing's house, 'St Brelades', in Surbiton.

generally a most affectionate little animal but she simply flew at me, biting my wrist all over before I could fasten the hutch. Our friendship is at present restored with scented soap!'

When Beatrix came back to London from the Lake District she found that Norman was away again. 'I should be very grateful if anyone could find time to write me a line how the "Tailor" is going on? I am afraid I am not making a good start yet with the rabbit book, I have been rather bothered but I hope it will come right; when will Mr Norman Warne be coming back? and able to look over it.' Beatrix was now making regular visits to the Warne office, Chandos House in Bedford Street, and it was only Norman that she wanted to see.

The Warnes were a closely-knit family and Norman was undoubtedly the favourite uncle to his growing number of nephews and nieces. He was a keen cyclist, and every Saturday morning he took his nephew, Fred, to play tennis at Fruing's house in Surbiton and most mornings they went for an early morning dip together in the Serpentine. When he was away on his selling trips to Blackpool or Huddersfield, Norman wrote long letters to his nieces, promising to visit them the moment he returned, 'I really think I shall have to start building a new doll's house if you dress such a lot of dolls and the newly married couple will certainly require a new house, as they can't very well reside with their Mother-in-law. In the latter case the furniture and windows would certainly be broken. The Boots has just come to say it is post time so I must close.'

The library of the Warnes' Bedford Square house, photographed in 1905 with Beatrix's little books lying on the table.

Beatrix was entranced by this large and happy Warne family, who congregated in Bedford Square at every excuse for a party, especially at Christmas. Winifred Warne, Fruing's daughter, remembers those parties well: 'The Warnes enjoyed each other's company. The parties were for the children and the grown-ups played games with us, but we were never noisy or rowdy together. On one particular occasion, when Uncle Norman dressed up as Father Christmas and my cousin Louie, who was a bold child, recognised him and went up and kissed him, the servants and nurses who were watching from an alcove remarked on her "very forward behaviour".' Beatrix and Millie became good friends, having a good deal in common, and before long Beatrix went to stay at Bedford Square so she could be included in the fun of a family party. 'I remember her coming to help me get dressed,' recalled Winifred, who was a small girl of four or five at the time. 'And she put my knickers on inside out. My nurse was fairly scathing about it, "These clever people don't know how to do simple things."'

Beatrix's books were doing well and by the end of 1903 over 50,000 copies of *Peter Rabbit* had been sold. 'The public must be fond of rabbits! What an appalling quantity of Peter.' The royalties were beginning to mount up and Beatrix made an arrangement to be paid by regular cheque each month. In November she asked Norman for that month's cheque to be very closely followed by the next one as she was about to buy a field in the Lake District, in the village of Sawrey which she had loved ever since the family had

(*above*) A sketch from the manuscript of *Benjamin Bunny*.

(*below*) Beatrix made a Peter Rabbit doll and registered it at the Patent Office in London on 28 December 1903.

spent the summer there some seven years before. She was working on 'the rabbit book', a sequel to *Peter Rabbit* about his cousin Benjamin Bunny, and she was making a Peter Rabbit doll. 'I am cutting out calico patterns of Peter, I have not got it right yet, but the expression is going to be lovely; especially the whiskers – (pulled out of a brush!). I think I will make one first of white velveteen painted, like those policeman dolls are made of; fur is very difficult to sew. I cannot tell what to do about those stories. At present I intend to make dolls; I think I could make him stand on his legs if he had some lead bullets in his feet!' When the doll was finished, she sent it to Norman to give to one of his nieces. 'I hope the little girl will like the doll. There is some shot in the body and coat tail. I don't think it will come out until the legs give way, children sometimes expect comfits out of animals, so I give fair warning!' She was keen for Norman to explore the possibilities of finding a manufacturer for it. 'I wish you could do something at once about the doll; Harrod's said they were bringing out a doll like the advt. of "Sunny Jim", there is a run on toys copied from pictures.' And Beatrix was aware that others were starting to benefit from the success of her books. 'My Father has just bought a squirrel in the Burlington Arcade, it was sold as "Nutkin"; it is prettier than the rabbits, but evidently the same make. I wonder how soon we may expect to see the mice!'

By now Beatrix had quite a collection of real animals and she still took them with her wherever she went, the hedgehog in a basket and the rabbits and mice in wooden boxes. 'I don't take any tickets for them.' She wrote to Winifred about her hedgehog in one of her special picture letters from Wales: 'My hedgehog Mrs Tiggy-winkle is a great traveller, I don't know how many journeys she hasn't done. She enjoys going by train, she is always very hungry when she is on a journey. The next journey will be quite a short one, I think I am going to the sea-side on Saturday. I wonder if I shall find any crabs and shells and shrimps. Mrs Tiggy-winkle won't eat shrimps; I think it is very silly of her, she will eat worms and beetles, and I am sure that shrimps would be much nicer. I think you must ask Mrs Tiggy-winkle to tea when she comes back to London later on, she will drink milk like anything, out of a doll's tea-cup!' One of her rabbits was called Josey, 'a dear rabbit, she is so tame; although she is only a common wild one, who lived in a rabbit hole under a hedge. A boy caught her when she was quite a baby, she could sit in my hand.' The mice, Tom Thumb and Hunca Munca, brought back from Gloucestershire earlier in the year when they were caught in the kitchen of Harescombe Grange, needed a new cage. Who better to make it than the man who built doll's houses for his nieces? 'I wish "Johnny Crow" would make my mouse "a little house"; do you think he would if I

the Sea-side on Saturday.

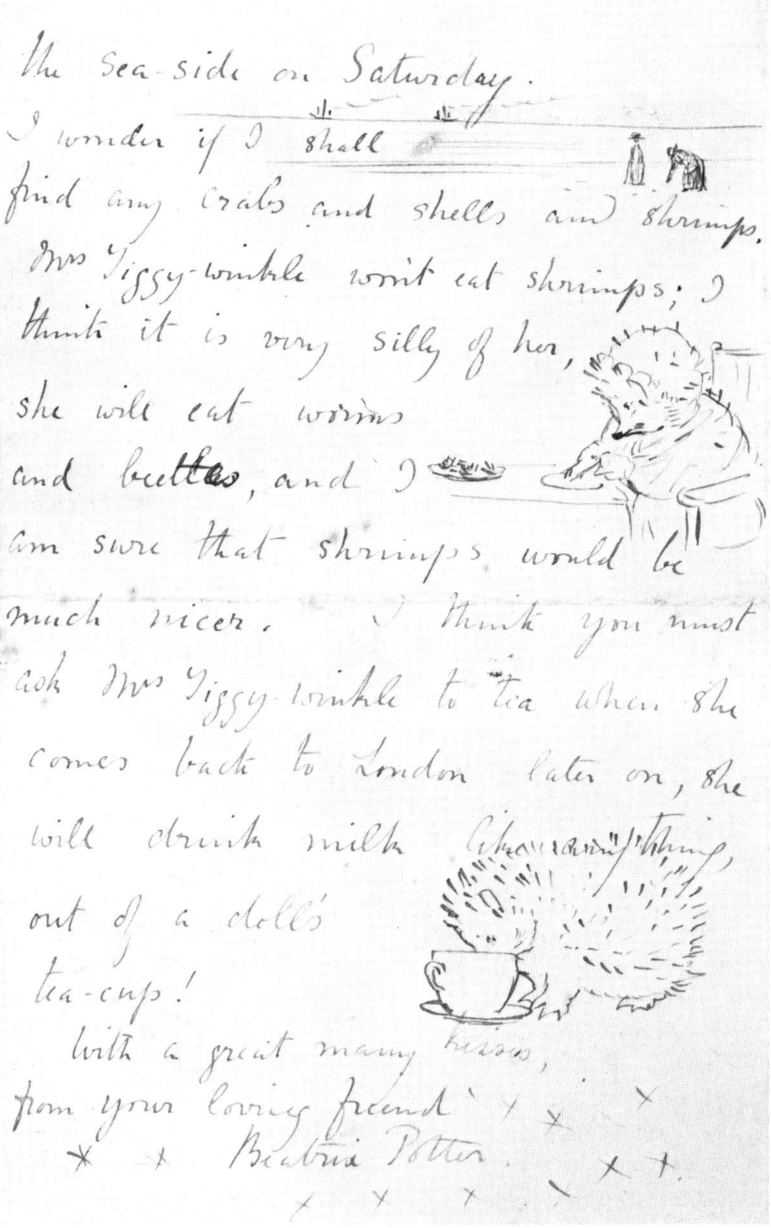

I wonder if I shall

find any crabs and shells and shrimps.

Mrs Tiggy-winkle won't eat shrimps; I

think it is very silly of her,

she will eat worms

and beetles, and I

am sure that shrimps would be

much nicer.   I think you must

ask Mrs Tiggy-winkle to tea when she

comes back to London later on, she

will drink milk like anything,

out of a doll's

tea-cup!

With a great many kisses,

from your loving friend

Beatrix Potter.

Beatrix always took her favourite animals away with her. She wrote to Winifred Warne from Wales on 6 September 1905 about her hedgehog, Mrs Tiggy-winkle.

made a paper plan? I want one with the glass at the side before I draw Hunca Munca again. Mine are apt to be ricketty!'

Beatrix had already nearly finished the book about Benjamin Bunny; the mice – and Norman's carpentry – were giving her the idea for the next book. Watching her mice carrying their treasures into their nest had sparked off a story about some mice raiding a doll's house while the dolls were out. As a model for the house she

(*above*) A sketch of Tom Thumb and Hunca Munca approaching the doll's house, from the manuscript of *The Tale of Two Bad Mice*.

(*right*) Winifred Warne's doll's house, made for her by Norman, was the model for the one in *The Tale of Two Bad Mice*.

would use the one Norman had made for Winifred, but it would mean going down to Surbiton to draw it. Norman and the Fruing Warnes were delighted with the idea and issued a warm invitation, but Mrs Potter was beginning to sense that her daughter's friendship with the Warne family had gone far enough and that the time had come to stop it. 'I was very much perplexed about the doll's-house,' wrote Beatrix to Norman. 'I would have gone gladly to draw it, and I should be so *very* sorry if Mrs Warne or you thought me uncivil. I did not think I could manage to go to Surbiton without staying to lunch; I hardly ever go out, and my mother is so "exacting" I had not enough spirit to say anything about it. I have felt vexed with myself since, but I did not know what to do. It does wear a person out ... As far as the book is concerned I think I can do it from the photograph and my box; but it is very hard to have seemed uncivil.'

Norman was naturally disappointed but set about helping Beatrix by sending photographs and by buying her dolls as models. 'Thank you so very much for the queer little dollies, they are just exactly what I wanted, and a curiosity – coming from Seven Dials ... I will provide a print dress and a smile for Jane; her little stumpy feet are so funny. I think I shall make a dear little book of it. I shall be glad to get done with the rabbits.' He sent her doll's house furniture to draw. 'I received the parcel from Hamley's this morning; the things will all do beautifully; the ham's appearance is enough to cause indigestion. I am getting almost more treasures than I can squeeze into one small book.' Norman then suggested that perhaps the solution might be for Mrs Potter to accompany Beatrix to Surbiton, but it was no good. 'I don't think that my mother would be very likely to want to go to Surbiton, you did not understand what I meant by "exacting". People who only see her casually do not know how disagreeable she can be when she takes dislikes. I should have been glad enough to go. I did not know what to do.' However, before the book was finished Beatrix did go to Surbiton. Winifred Warne recalls her visit, 'She had lunch with my mother and was afterwards shown the doll's house in our nursery. She examined the house carefully and borrowed the policeman doll to copy. I remember wondering whether she would send it back. She did! She was dressed very severely in a dark coat and skirt, with a highly-polished brown leather belt and men's shoes. She had a man's umbrella, which she left in the nursery and my father took it back to the office the next day.'

The Tale of Two Bad Mice, dedicated to 'W.M.L.W. the little girl who had the doll's house', and *The Tale of Benjamin Bunny*, 'for the children of Sawrey from old Mr Bunny', were both published in September 1904. There was a rather critical review of *Benjamin Bunny* in *The Times Literary Supplement* – 'Among the little books which have become as much a manifestation of autumn as falling leaves, one looks first for whatever Miss Beatrix Potter gives ... In her new book ... although there is no diminution in the charm and drollery of the drawings, Miss Potter's fancy is not what it was. The story is inconclusive. Next year we think she must call in a literary assistant. We have no hesitation in calling her pencil perfect.' By the end of the year there were 30,000 copies of each of the new books in print.

1904 had been another busy year for Beatrix. Among other things, she was now a godmother. In November 1903 Annie Moore had given birth to her eighth child, and when she christened the girl Beatrix Annie's friend agreed at once to be a godmother. She gave the new baby a silver sugar bowl engraved 'BM 3rd Nov 1903', which is still treasured by Beatrix Moore today.

Meanwhile, in Bolton Gardens, Beatrix Potter was enjoying the

A sketch of Lucinda and Jane, the dolls in *The Tale of Two Bad Mice*, which were bought for Beatrix by Norman Warne.

Annie Moore's eighth child was born in November 1903 and christened Beatrix after her godmother.

(*above*) Beatrix was commissioned to design the Frederick Warne 1904–5 catalogue cover for the princely sum of £2.

Lucie's cottage, Little-town, nestling into the side of Cat Bells, looks much the same in 1985 (*right*) as it did when drawn by Beatrix in 1904 (*opposite*) for her new book about 'an excellent clear-starcher', *The Tale of Mrs Tiggy-winkle*.

knowledge that perhaps one day she could be independent – 'It is pleasant to feel I could earn my own living.' As well as working on the two new books, she had designed a cover for the next Warne catalogue – for the princely sum of £2: and she had made Peter Rabbit dolls and invented a Peter Rabbit board game. She had also refused Warne's request to illustrate someone else's book and turned away an approach from Longmans to write a reader for elementary schools: 'I have a strong feeling that every outside book which I did, would prevent me from finishing one of my own. I enjoy inventing stories – any number – but I draw so slowly & laboriously, that there are sure to be favourites of my own left undone at the end of my working life-time, whether short or long.'

The question was what book to do next? The answer lay once again in a story that Beatrix had written for a particular child some years earlier while staying at Lingholm, a story about a hedgehog, Mrs Tiggy-winkle, who was a washerwoman. The washerwoman at Dalguise, Kitty MacDonald, was undoubtedly the inspiration for Mrs Tiggy-winkle, and Lucie Carr, one of the daughters of the vicar of Newlands in the valley that runs to the west of Cat Bells, near Lingholm in the Lake District, was the Lucie in the book. Beatrix had her hedgehog model with her to draw whenever she had a moment, even when she went to stay in Wales, 'I am accompanied by Mrs Tiggy – carefully concealed – my aunt cannot endure animals,' and of course in London, 'Mrs Tiggy as a model is comical; so long as she can go to sleep on my knee she is delighted, but if she is propped up on end for half an hour, she first begins to yawn pathetically, and then she *does* bite! Nevertheless she is a dear person; just like a very fat, rather stupid little dog.'

Norman gave all the encouragement he could and the new book began to take shape, with Beatrix reporting progress every few days. 'The hedgehog drawings are turning out very comical. I have dressed up a cotton wool dummy figure for convenience of drawing the clothes. It is such a little figure of fun; it terrifies my rabbit; but Hunca Munca is always at pulling out the stuffing.'

Beatrix was also designing Peter Rabbit and Benjamin Bunny wallpaper, wrestling with the problems of matching up the joins and whether to accept Sanderson's fee of £10 or to offer them to Liberty instead. She was anxious to follow her previous pattern of working on two books at a time, starting a new book when well into the first in order to vary the subject of her drawing, and once again she suggested to Norman that she do the book about Jeremy Fisher: 'I'm afraid you don't like frogs but it would make pretty pictures with water-forget-me-nots, lilies, etc.' In the end it was an

For *The Tale of Mrs Tiggy-winkle* Beatrix made numerous sketches of her own pet hedgehog.

(*left*) An unfinished pen-and-ink and water-colour study of Mrs Tiggy-winkle, with Lucie sketched in pencil.

entirely different idea that won approval, a book about a Pomeranian dog called Duchess, a cat called Ribby, and a rather special pie with the crust held up by a patty-pan.

The person to whom Beatrix regularly turned for support and the one who always gave her the most encouragement was Norman. He deeply admired this strong-willed and spirited woman with her amazing talent for producing bestsellers. They exchanged letters nearly every day, still couched in the most formal of terms, but their friendship had deepened. One day, in the summer of 1905, Norman proposed marriage. 'It was the strangest of courtships,' comments Winifred Warne, who remembers family discussions about it years afterwards. 'They were never alone together. When Beatrix went to the office she was always chaperoned and when she went to Bedford Square some other member of the family would always be there, too, though Millie was more of a help than a hindrance. Norman even proposed to Beatrix by letter.'

Beatrix was overjoyed by Norman's proposal but there was one big obstacle – her parents, and in particular her mother. As far as the Potters knew, their daughter's relationship with Norman Warne was solely one of author and publisher, though there had been that time when they had had to prevent Beatrix from going off to draw with him somewhere in Surbiton. Now they were presented with this extraordinary proposal, that their beloved Beatrix should marry 'into trade', and they were not pleased. In fact they did everything they could to prevent it.

Beatrix on the other hand was quite determined. She would shortly be thirty-nine years old and, while she acknowledged that a loyal daughter's duty was to respect her parents' wishes, she accepted this kind and gentle man's proposal in the face of her parents'

Two sketches from the manuscript of *The Tale of Mrs Tiggy-winkle*.

This sketch for *The Pie and the Patty-pan* of Duchess and Ribby having tea was inscribed 'Is it a pie made of mouse?'

disapproval. She insisted that she would wear his engagement ring but she agreed that no one beyond the two immediate families would be told about the arrangement for the moment, not even Norman's two brothers in the firm.

It was a difficult and emotional time for Beatrix, hardly conducive to getting books ready for publication, but she battled on. *The Tale of Mrs Tiggy-winkle* was nearly finished, though the text was giving trouble: 'She is supposed to be exorcising spots and iron stains, same as Lady Macbeth(!)' *The Pie and the Patty-pan* was also taking longer than she had planned – 'I think the book runs some risk of being over-cooked if it goes on much longer!' – but both books were completed and delivered to Norman before the summer holidays began. *Mrs Tiggy-winkle* she dedicated to 'The real little Lucie of Newlands', and *The Pie and the Patty-pan* she dedicated to Annie Moore's sixth child, Joan, though with her god-daughter, Beatrix, in mind: 'For Joan, to read to Baby.'

Hunca Munca was one of Beatrix's pet mice, for whom Norman Warne made a new travelling box.

Beatrix was planning to visit her uncle in Wales and she needed Norman's help. 'It is Hunca Munca's travelling box that is shaky, it seems a shame to ask for joinering when it is such fine evenings, but perhaps it would not take so long to mend, I had so very much pleasure from her other little house.' Norman was pleased to help and he made Beatrix a new box for Hunca Munca – but the mouse never went to Wales. 'I cannot forgive myself for letting her tumble. I do miss her. She fell off the chandelier, she managed to stagger up the staircase into your little house, but she died in my hand about 10 minutes after. I think if I had broken my own neck it would have saved a deal of trouble.'

Just before she left for Wales herself, Beatrix had planned to deliver the first proofs of the new books to Norman. However, she discovered at the last moment that Norman was ill and that she would have to see Harold instead. Although Harold now knew about the engagement, Beatrix was keen that there should be no reference to it when they met and she hastily wrote him a letter. 'I will call on Monday morning at the office; I shall bring Miss Florrie Hammond with me. You will not think me very cross if I say I would rather *not* talk *yet* about that business? though I am *very glad* you have been told. I do trust that your brother is not going to be very ill, I got scared before he went to Manchester, wondering if he had been drinking bad water. I shall be able to ask you after his health, as Miss Florrie is not quite "all there" and

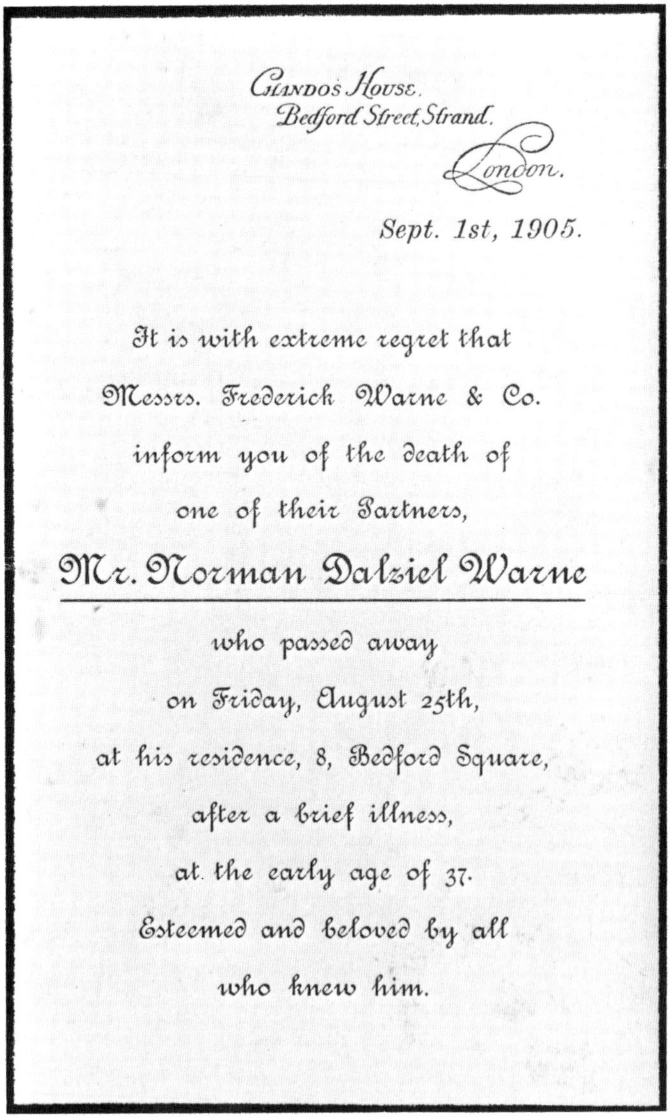

> Chandos House,
> Bedford Street, Strand.
> London.
>
> Sept. 1st, 1905.
>
> It is with extreme regret that
>
> Messrs. Frederick Warne & Co.
>
> inform you of the death of
>
> one of their Partners,
>
> **Mr. Norman Dalziel Warne**
>
> who passed away
>
> on Friday, August 25th,
>
> at his residence, 8, Bedford Square,
>
> after a brief illness,
>
> at the early age of 37.
>
> Esteemed and beloved by all
>
> who knew him.

Only a few months after Beatrix accepted Norman's proposal of marriage, he died of pernicious anaemia.

stone-deaf!' She referred again to the engagement: 'It is a very awkward way of happening; I think he is going a little too fast now that he has started; but I trust it may come right in the end.'

Three weeks later Norman was still ill and his mother, on her eightieth birthday, wrote to one of her grandchildren of the family's concern, 'I wish dear Norman was getting better, but it is very slow work. He is so weak and cannot take anything but milk. He keeps very cheerful for all that but he can scarcely stand.' Five days later, on 25 August 1905, Norman Dalziel Warne died of pernicious anaemia in his home in Bedford Square. He was buried in Highgate Cemetery, after a funeral service which began with the

Shortly after Norman's death, his sister-in-law, Mary, sent Beatrix this photograph of his favourite nieces, Winifred and Eveline.

hymn, 'There is a land of pure delight' and ended with, 'For all the saints who from their labours rest.' He was only thirty-seven.

Norman's death was almost more than Beatrix could bear, particularly as she was unable to talk about it outside the family, for no one else knew that she had even been engaged to him, but the Warnes were a great support and a month after the funeral Beatrix was invited to stay at No. 8 Bedford Square. From there she wrote to Fruing Warne's wife, Mary, thanking her for a photograph she had sent of Winifred and her baby sister, Eveline: 'I should have liked it and admired it even if they had been strangers, but I have heard Norman talk so often about the children that they seem like little friends ... I cannot tell you how grateful I have felt for the kindness of all of you, it has been a real comfort and pleasure to stay in this house. Millie and I went up to Highgate yesterday, the stone is put back quite neatly again; it seems to want something planting at the back, there is much untidy trampled earth where the hawthorn was cut down. I don't believe grass will ever grow well under the fir tree. I was wondering whether Japanese anemonies would grow where it is rather shaded. Millie says you have them in your garden and know their habits.'

Beatrix began writing regularly to Millie, too, a correspondence that was to last for the rest of Beatrix's life, and of Norman she wrote, 'He did not live long, but he fulfilled a useful happy life. I must try to make a fresh beginning next year.' Her immediate plans were to return to North Wales to continue sketching, 'which has got sadly neglected this summer', and then to go up to the Lake District for a short holiday. She had her work in which to try to lose herself and her grief, and she was also determined that somehow she must get away altogether from London with all its sad associations.

Harold Warne took over as Beatrix's editor at the office in Bedford Street, and Beatrix, anxious to have something to work on while she was in the Lake District, wondered if perhaps he could be persuaded to let her do Jeremy Fisher at last? 'We had thought

(*below*) The first book Beatrix worked on with Norman's brother, Harold, was *The Tale of Mr Jeremy Fisher*. These are two early sketches for the book, the one on the right from the manuscript illustrates 'Mr Jeremy liked getting his feet wet'.

PLATE XIV (above) The beach at Sidmouth in Devon, where Beatrix was on holiday with her parents in April 1902.

PLATE XV (right) An interior at Gwaynynog, Denbigh, March 1904, the home of Beatrix's Uncle Fred Burton.

PLATE XVI Hill Top Farm
was bought by Beatrix in
1905 with her royalties and
a small legacy.

PLATE XVII Kep, Beatrix's
favourite of all the dogs on
the farm, March 1909.

PLATE XVIII (right) 'Nutkin sat upon a beech-stump playing marbles.' An early study for *Squirrel Nutkin*, 1903.

PLATE XIX (below) Harvest time at Esthwaite Water, looking over the lake from Sawrey to the Coniston Fells.

PLATE XX Mrs Ribby 'sat down before the fire to wait for the little dog'.
An unfinished painting for *The Pie and the Patty-pan*, 1905.

The boat was round and
green, and very like the
other lily-leaves. It was
moored tethered to a water plant
in the middle of the pond.

22

20

An opening from the
manuscript of *Mr Jeremy
Fisher*, showing 'tethered'
changed to 'moored'. For the
final text it was changed again
to 'tied'.

of doing the larger half-crown book of verses *Appley Dapply* and
the frog *Mr Jeremy Fisher* to carry on the series of little ones. I
know some people don't like frogs but I think I had convinced
Norman that I could make a really pretty book with a good many
flowers and water plants for backgrounds. That book would be
easy and plain sailing ... I think unless anything went wrong at
home, I shall stay away two months; but I shall want to come to
London in the middle of the time to get the projected new books
looked over, and to see dear Millie again. I feel as if my work and
your kindness will be my greatest comfort ... It will be a trying
thing to come for the first time to the office but there is no help
for it.'

Earlier that summer Beatrix had added to her property in the
Lake District, sinking all her savings and also a small legacy she
had received into a working farm in Near Sawrey called Hill
Top. When she bought it the farm was in the capable hands of

An unfinished drawing by
Beatrix of Hill Top, the farm
she bought in Sawrey in the
summer of 1905.

John Cannon and his wife, and Beatrix asked him to stay on to
manage the farm for her. It was time she went to see how things
were going. She found the village amused by this strange new
owner of Hill Top, an 'off-comer' from London – 'My purchase
seems to be regarded as a huge joke; I have been going over my hill
with a tape measure,' – and she discovered that discussing the
details of pig farming and checking the accuracy of the farm's
butter scales were ideal distractions from the hurt and sorrow of
Norman's death. There was also book work to be done: 'I have
been drawing a frog today with a fishing-rod. I think it is going to
be a funny book.' Harold Warne had agreed that *The Tale of Mr
Jeremy Fisher* should be published at last, in the summer of 1906.
At the same time, Beatrix was working on ideas for a number of
books for much younger children than the ones who enjoyed the
stories in her 'little books'. She planned to tell these new tales
almost entirely in pictures, with only a brief text, and to have each
one made up in a panoramic form folded into a wallet in concer-
tina style, so that it could be pulled out and looked at in one long
strip like a frieze. The first book was about a bad rabbit and had
been written as a present the previous Christmas for Harold's
daughter, Louie, after she told Aunt Beatrix that she thought Peter
was much too good and that she wanted a story about a really
naughty rabbit. The companion book was about a cat who was
proving to be 'an exasperating model . . . I have borrowed a Kitten

and I am rather glad of the opportunity of working at the drawings. It is very young and pretty and a most fearful pickle. One of the mason's brought it from Windermere.' *The Story of a Fierce Bad Rabbit* and *The Story of Miss Moppet* were published in time for Christmas 1906.

The year had been another busy one for Beatrix. She loved the Lake District almost as much as her beloved Scotland, the ever-changing colours of the hillsides, the quiet waters of the tarns and lakes, the sound of the wind in the larches and the bubbling cries of the curlews in summer. She must find a way to spend more time there and she must have somewhere more permanent to live than lodgings in the village. There was not enough room for her and the Cannons at Hill Top, and anyway she needed them there; the only

(*above*) Two sketches from the manuscript for the book version of *The Story of Miss Moppet*, with the editorial comment that the cat is now thinner than she was in the panorama.

The Story of Miss Moppet was first published as a panorama for younger children for Christmas 1906.

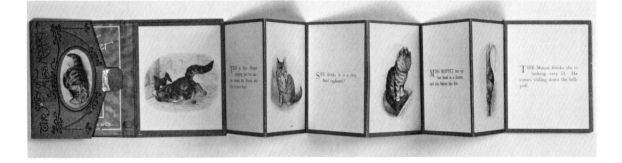

solution was to expand the farmhouse to accommodate them all. By the end of the following summer the alterations at Hill Top were finished. There were separate quarters for the Cannons and the main part of the house for Beatrix, and both Millie Warne and Beatrix's old friend from the museum, Gertrude Woodward, made the journey to Sawrey to see her new acquisition and to share her enthusiasm for the house and the garden. Beatrix was not able to spend more than a month out of the year at Hill Top, as she was still very much tied to her parents and felt she must be on hand when they called upon her, but she went to Sawrey for a few days whenever she could get away. She had just turned forty and a whole new life was opening before her. Now both the children of Helen and Rupert Potter had become farmers.

Hill Top Farm started to expand quite quickly. Late in the summer John Cannon had bought some sheep, 'sixteen ewes so there will be lambs next spring'. They were Herdwick sheep, native to the Lake District, a hardy breed that thrives on the high fells and with wool prized for its hardwearing and waterproof qualities, particularly for clothing and carpets. A few years before, the increasing use of linoleum for floor covering had caused the price of Herdwick wool to slump and many farmers had been forced to turn to other breeds of sheep not necessarily suitable for the fells. Some farmers had given up fell farming altogether, and there had been considerable concern that when farms on the high fells were abandoned the land would deteriorate and the landscape irrevocably change. Beatrix's friend and admirer, Canon Rawnsley, was characteristically in the forefront of the campaign to re-establish the old breed of sheep, and he founded the Herdwick Sheepbreeders Association in 1899. He also successfully convinced

Rupert Potter was still taking delayed action photographs when he and his wife were staying at Lingholm on 3 September 1907.

Beatrix now had sixteen Herdwick sheep at Hill Top Farm. The premier show for Herdwicks is still held at Eskdale, Cumbria.

Beatrix that now she was a farmer she should play her part in bringing Herdwicks back to the fells. Within two years Hill Top Farm had over thirty Herdwicks – and ten cows, fourteen pigs and some ducks and hens. Beatrix had been interested in sheep for a long time, and in the sketchbook that she kept during her stay at Fawe Park in 1903 she had noted in meticulous detail the markings of the sheep from the farms in all the surrounding areas – and with the sheep came sheepdogs. There had always been dogs in Beatrix's life, first Sandy and then Spot, and now her growing involvement in sheep breeding began her deep attachment to collies. The dogs on the farm were working dogs, living outside and totally dedicated to their work, but Beatrix always had one dog which was especially hers. Kep was the first of a long line of collies, as devoted to his mistress as she was to him.

Although her new-found enthusiasms were taking up more and more of her attention, Beatrix continued to work on her 'little

books', and she used her animals and property to the full as models and as source material. *The Tale of Tom Kitten*, published in September 1907, was set in the house and garden of Hill Top and in the village of Sawrey, and Tom Kitten's mother was named after the cat in the house where Beatrix used to stay: 'Mrs S had got a new kitten called Tabitha Twitchit.' As her model for Tom she still had her drawings of the mason's cat she had borrowed from Windermere, and she dedicated the book 'to all Pickles, – especially to those that get upon my garden wall'. Beatrix had a disagreement with Harold Warne about part of the text when he criticised the line 'all the rest of Tom's clothes came off'. He suggested that she should change it to 'nearly all' instead, presumably worried that some people might be offended. Beatrix was irritated. '"Nearly all" won't do! because I have drawn Thomas already with nothing! That would not signify; I could gum something over but there are not many garments for Mr Drake to dress himself in; and it would give the story a new and criminal aspect if he forcibly took off and *stole* Tom's trousers!'

Beatrix's next book was *The Tale of Jemima Puddle-duck*, to be published in the summer of 1908, and into it she put her favourite dog, Kep. The setting is the farm at Hill Top and the surrounding

(*opposite*) Whenever she could be spared from looking after her parents, Beatrix spent her time at Hill Top.

Bertram, though secretly married and farming in Ancrum, occasionally joined the family on holiday. Rupert Potter photographed his two children together on 3 September 1908.

Few early sketches for *The Tale of Jemima Puddle-duck* have survived. This pencil sketch (*above left*) and pen-and-ink drawing (*above right*) were intended for *Jemima Puddle-duck's Painting Book* which was to come in 1925.

village; Jemima was one of the farm ducks who was always looking for somewhere else to lay her eggs. John Cannon was still the manager of Hill Top Farm and *Jemima Puddle-duck* was for his children, 'A farmyard tale for Ralph and Betsy'. Beatrix had drawn them into one of the pictures and their mother into another.

The Roly-poly Pudding, later to be called *The Tale of Samuel Whiskers*, was also set at Hill Top. Though it was not published until October 1908, the story had been written soon after Beatrix first bought the farm and discovered that the house was overrun with rats. She wrote to Millie about her battle with them. 'The rats have come back in great force, two big ones were trapped in the shed here, beside turning out a nest of eight baby rats in the cucumber frame opposite the door. They are getting at the corn at the farm. Mrs Cannon calmly announced that she should get four or five cats! Imagine my feelings; but I daresay they will live in the outbuildings.' And a week later, 'The cats have not arrived yet, but Mrs Cannon has seen a rat sitting up eating its dinner under the kitchen table in the middle of the afternoon. We are putting zinc on the bottoms of the doors – that and cement skirtings will puzzle them.' Those who know the book will be aware that the cats when they arrived did the trick but now and then a rat did return to Hill Top, as Beatrix recounted in a letter to Winifred Warne. 'I was sitting very quiet before the fire in the library reading a book, and I heard someone pitter patter along the passage, and then someone scratched at the outside of the library door. I thought it was the puppy or the kitten so I took no notice. But next morning we discovered that Mr Whiskers had been in the house! We could not find him anywhere, so we think he had got in – and out again – by squeezing under a door. He had stolen the very oddest thing! There is a sort of large cupboard or closet where I do my photographing, it is papered inside with rather a pretty green and gold paper; and Samuel had torn off strips of paper all round the closet as high as he could reach up. I could see the marks of his little teeth! Every scrap was taken away. I wonder what in the world he wanted it for? I think Anna Maria must have been there, with him, to help, and I think she must have wanted to paper her best sitting room! I only wonder she did not take the paste brush, which was on the shelf in the closet.'

The dedication for *The Roly-poly Pudding* is to Beatrix's own pet rat of many years before, 'In remembrance of "Sammy", The intelligent pink-eyed Representative of a Persecuted (but Irrepressible) Race, An affectionate little Friend, and most accomplished thief.' It was the same Sammy who had caused a certain unease when Beatrix had taken him to stay in Wales with her: 'I have

(*below left*) An early pencil sketch for *The Roly-poly Pudding*, published in 1908. In 1926 the title was changed to *The Tale of Samuel Whiskers*.

(*below right*) Beatrix wrote to Winifred Warne from Sidmouth on 29 December 1906, with an account of how Samuel Whiskers stole some wallpaper.

memory of him waddling along the floor, waiting to be picked up by my Aunt – a stout elderly lady who did not altogether appreciate his friendly advances. Poor Sammy. White rats are not very long lived; and he was always wanting to be petted in his declining months – But not everybody liked him – One of his scrapes was to cut a neat round piece, size of our half crowns, out of the middle of a sheet. He carried a curious collection of stolen articles to his box. I remember the Aunt providing a hard boiled egg, and watching the rolling of the egg along a passage; but she requested that his neat box might be kept firmly fastened.'

The books were now starting to earn quite a lot of money and there were a growing number of merchandise off-shoots, based on the characters in the books. On each sale Beatrix was paid a royalty. There were china tea-sets and figurines, a Peter Rabbit game, and wooden Peter Rabbits; there were plans for a Peter Rabbit painting book and a Jemima Puddle-duck doll. Beatrix was closely involved in every transaction and showed herself to be a keen businesswoman. With the money she earned she bought new stock for the farm, laid on water to Hill Top and purchased more land.

In the early months of 1909 Beatrix put the finishing touches to a sequel to *Peter Rabbit* and *Benjamin Bunny*. 'I have done lots of sketches – not at all to the purpose – and will now endeavour to finish up the F. Bunnies without further delay.' *The Tale of the*

By 1907 Peter Rabbit was appearing in many forms. Beatrix herself devised The Game of Peter Rabbit.

Flopsy Bunnies had for its setting the garden of her uncle's house, Gwaynynog, which Beatrix had sketched many times since her first visit nearly fourteen years before. 'The garden is very large, two-thirds surrounded by a red-brick wall with many apricots, and an inner circle of old grey apple trees on wooden espaliers. It is very productive but not tidy, the prettiest kind of garden, where bright old fashioned flowers grow amongst the currant bushes.' The book was finished in March, and by the time it was delivered to Warne Beatrix was already at work on the next one, *Ginger and Pickles* (later changed to *The Tale of Ginger and Pickles*). Like *The Fierce Bad Rabbit*, this was a story that had first been written for Louie Warne as a Christmas present, and Beatrix had put into it a crowd of familiar characters from her earlier books – the two dolls Lucinda and Jane, Peter Rabbit and his family, Samuel Whiskers, Jeremy Fisher, Mrs Tiggy-winkle and Jemima Puddle-duck can all be found in the pictures. The story is set in and around the village shop in Sawrey, which at the time ruffled the feathers of some of the inhabitants: 'The "Ginger Pickle" book has been causing amusement, it has got a good many views which can be recognised in the village which is what they like, they are all quite jealous of each other's houses and cats getting into a book.' *The Tale of the*

(above left) The Tale of the Flopsy Bunnies was set in the garden of Gwaynynog, Uncle Fred Burton's house in Denbigh. The book *(above right)* was the sequel to *Peter Rabbit* and *Benjamin Bunny* and was published in July 1909.

A drawing from the manuscript of *Ginger and Pickles*, published in October 1909, into which Beatrix put many of the characters from her earlier books.

Flopsy Bunnies was published in July 1909, followed by *Ginger and Pickles* in October.

The following months saw Beatrix's first personal involvement in politics. All her life she had been close to the political scene, her grandfather and her uncle Members of Parliament, John Bright and Richard Cobden almost part of the family; as a child she had heard discussions and campaign plans for a free trade policy, and as a young woman she had witnessed Hardwicke Rawnsley's fight against it. Tariff reform was to be one of the issues of the 1910 general election, and here was something about which Beatrix felt strongly, for the present free trade policy was affecting her personally. A Peter Rabbit doll was being manufactured in Germany because no one could be found in Britain to match the price, and there was the distinct possibility that it might be cheaper to print her books in the United States and to ship them into Britain, rather than originate them in her own country. This was something that Beatrix would not stand for, particularly as some years before the Americans had 'pirated' Peter Rabbit, losing her the copyright there and therefore all income on any sales. She would do all she could to campaign for tariff reform. She contributed posters, in both picture and in verse, lamenting the death of the South London toy trade:

> When a Workman ain't got any Wages –
> Now what is the good of 'cheap' bread,
> While you argue and talks and rampages –
> Poor Camberwell Dolly lies dead!

She wrote leaflets complaining on behalf of farmers and small-holders of the plans to raise land taxes. She attacked the Liberal

When a Workman ain't got any Wages —
Now what is the good of "cheap" bread?
While you argues and talks and rampages —
Poor Camberwell Dolly lies dead!

THE SHORTAGE OF HORSES.

ON Feb. 25th certain questions were asked in the House of Commons about a **census of horses**. Papers have recently been distributed and collected by the country police. Probably many farmers believed, (as I did,) that the census fore-shadowed some welcome scheme for encouraging horse-breeding, or for subsidising yeomanry remounts. **Such schemes are constantly advocated by Unionist Members.**

On Feb. 25th Capt. Faber (Unionist, W. Hampshire) asked the Home Secretary (Mr. Winston

Government's recent census of horses, which they had assured the owners was not for taxation purposes or for use by the military authorities but which was in reality just that – for the conscription of horses 'in a great national emergency'.

In all this she was supported by Harold Warne, who helped her to draft the leaflets and sent them to be printed; many of the posters she drew herself by hand. She made personal approaches to publishers and printers for their support on the question of copyright protection and import restrictions, and with the help of Margaret Hammond, the niece of her first governess, she addressed hundreds of envelopes, sending out leaflets the length and breadth of the country – 'My fingers are tired of writing.' To Beatrix's disappointment the Liberal Government was returned with a working majority, but 'I am much rejoiced to see the results of the neighbouring Windermere and Kendal elections. I promise faithfully to return to pigs and mice next week.'

On New Year's Day 1910 Beatrix had given to Harold's daughter, Nellie, a story about a woodmouse, 'a most terribly tidy particular little mouse', and this was to be Beatrix's next book, but she was finding that the demands on her time when on her fleeting

(*above left*) Beatrix actively campaigned for tariff reform during the run-up to the 1910 general election. And in the same year, signing her leaflet 'North Country Farmer', she attacked the Liberal Government's census of horses (*above right*).

The story of Mrs Tittlemouse was a New Year gift to Harold Warne's daughter, Nellie, in 1910. An early sketch (*above left*) in which Beatrix drew an earwig instead of a beetle and (*above right*) the manuscript sketch of Mrs Tittlemouse discovering Mr Jackson.

trips to the Lake District were slowing up her usually fast schedule: 'I had three hard working days at Sawrey but could do no sketching.' She was also still much concerned with her parents, always accompanying them on their regular spring and summer holidays to Teignmouth and to Sidmouth, and often to Windermere. They were not entirely sympathetic to her frequent absences at Hill Top, but they were reluctant to go there with her. 'I don't like leaving my parents for any length of time, they were both very well in health but they do not like this place so they feel inclined to be dull here. It is a fine view, but such a *hill*!' For the first time for some years there would be only one new book by Beatrix Potter in the Warne Christmas catalogue, *The Tale of Mrs Tittlemouse*, which was published in October 1910. The pig book that Beatrix had in mind would have to be done another time: 'I cannot screw anything out of my head at present! I have done a little sketching when it does not rain, and I spent a very wet hour *inside* the pig stye drawing the pig. It tries to nibble my boots, which is interrupting. I don't think it ever answers to try and finish a book in summer.'

chapter four

'The publisher is a gentleman who prints
books, and he wants a bigger book than he
has got enough money to pay for!'

Beatrix photographed by her father in 1912

Beatrix now had sixteen books in print with Frederick Warne. She was their most important author and her books were making the firm a considerable amount of money. Though she could never have the same relationship with Harold that she had had with Norman, Beatrix liked him and was fond of his family, particularly his children. She was also fond of Fruing Warne and often visited his family and wrote regularly to the children. They all gave her presents at Christmas: 'Excuse me mentioning it but for goodness sake don't give me anything *big*! The log scuttle has been much admired but it was the last straw for squeezing in. I know you always leave your shopping to the last, if you don't know what to get I should much appreciate a book, is not there a book of Irish poetry just published by the Oxford U. press called the Dublin Anthology, I don't think it would harm me, though doubtless full of treason. I wish Frue would give me a book about pruning roses; there is nothing like being candid. You will receive pork, killed today Monday, and very small.'

Everything was going well on a personal basis at Warne but something was bothering Beatrix, and she was beginning to feel uneasy. The arrangement that had been made with Norman

Another Potter family photograph. Rupert, Bertram and Beatrix were staying at Lindeth How on 4 August 1911.

whereby she received a monthly cheque from the firm had continued, and there had always been the extra cheque whenever she needed money for a particular purchase, but there were now puzzling delays in the arrival of her money and there were complaints to her from hopeful toy manufacturers that their letters had remained unanswered. Beatrix was becoming impatient with Harold and with the way he was handling certain aspects of her affairs. 'I should very much prefer to manage the dolls myself, in future . . . I must ask you *not to make any fresh arrangements* without letting me know, I am seriously provoked about things being in such a muddle.' She was not worried about the way her books were produced, for she was looked after in that direction by Mr W. A. Herring, the production manager who had been with the company since 1894; it was the financial side that was giving her concern. Throughout the next four years Beatrix was constantly having to nag Harold about payment, 'I must confess I sometimes regret the times when cheques were smaller but *punctual*.' When Harold was away she wrote to Fruing, 'Would you mind telling me – without sentiment – and I trust without the slightest irritation – does FW & Co. mean to pay the first installment of the 1910 royalties . . . The difficulties of getting cheques at the time promised has sometimes rather perplexed and alarmed me.' It was becoming urgent for Beatrix to find out exactly what was happening.

Meanwhile she continued to produce her books, just one a year, *The Tale of Timmy Tiptoes* in 1911 and *The Tale of Mr Tod* in

(*above*) Hill Top Farm was extended to provide separate accommodation for Beatrix and her farm manager. Rupert photographed Beatrix's dresser in September 1912.

(*below*) Mr W. A. Herring who supervised the production of Beatrix's books at Frederick Warne from the beginning.

'Once upon a time there was a little fat comfortable grey squirrel.' The manuscript sketch (*above left*) and the finished illustration (*above right*) for *The Tale of Timmy Tiptoes*, published in October 1911.

(*right*) The black bear and the chipmunks in *Timmy Tiptoes* were specially chosen by Beatrix for her many American readers.

1912. From the many letters she received, Beatrix was conscious that she had a considerable following in America, and in *Timmy Tiptoes* she introduced characters that would be easily recognisable by American children who, after all, had never had the opportunity of even seeing a hedgehog. Mr and Mrs Chippy Hackee were chipmunks, and there was a bear about which Beatrix made a special note on her manuscript: 'I intended to represent the American black bear, it has a smooth coat like a sealskin coat.' *Timmy Tiptoes* is dedicated to 'many unknown little friends, including Monica'. 'I do not know the child,' Beatrix wrote, 'she is the school friend of a little cousin, who asked for it as a favour, and the name took my fancy.'

October 1911 also saw the publication of *Peter Rabbit's Painting Book*, a project that had been in preparation for three or four years but which Beatrix had never managed to finish. As well as black-and-white outlines to colour in, with softly colour-washed

You will want a Brush
and 5 Paints ———
   Antwerp Blue
   Crimson Lake
   Gamboge
   Sap Green and
   Burnt Sienna

You can mix
Blue with the Sienna
to make dark Brown.
Don't put the Brush in your
mouth. If you do, you will be
ill, like Peter.

Copyright 1911
by
FREDERICK WARNE & C°

Entered at Stationers Hall

PRINTED IN GREAT BRITAIN

Beatrix urged Warne to issue sheets of *Peter Rabbit's Painting Book* separately so that children could display their finished work.

A preliminary pen-and-ink drawing for *The Tale of Mr Tod*, a longer story with fewer colour pictures, published in 1912.

pictures as examples to follow, she included a few helpful hints for the young painter. 'You can mix blue with Sienna to make Dark Brown. Don't put the Brush in your mouth. If you do, you will be ill, like Peter.'

The manuscript of *The Tale of Mr Tod* was sent to Harold Warne in November 1911, though Beatrix had written the story some time before, setting it in the hills around Sawrey. In response to Harold's criticism of the hero's name, she hastened to point out its origin: '"Tod" is surely a very common name for fox? It is probably Saxon, it was the word in ordinary use in Scotland a few years ago, probably is still amongst country people. In the same way "brock" or "gray" is the country name for badger. I should call them "brocks" – both names are used in Westmoreland. "Brockholes" and "Graythwaite" are examples of place names; also Broxbourne and Brockhampton . . . "Hey quoth the Tod/its a braw bright night!/The wind's in the west/and the moon shines bright" – mean to say you never heard that?' She also thought that he might be concerned about her using the name of one of her fields in the story. 'I intirely forgot to ask you this morning whether you – (or Mrs Grundy) object to the name of Bull Banks? One thinks nothing about bulls and tups in the farming world; but after you objected to cigars it occurred to me to wonder. "Bull Banks" is a fine-sounding name, but I could just as well say "Oat-meal crag".'

Mr Tod was a longer story than usual and Beatrix provided fewer colour pictures for it than for her previous books; instead she drew a series of black-and-white line drawings so that there would be a picture for each page. She dedicated *Mr Tod* to the infant son of her cousin, Caroline Hutton, who had married the Laird of Ulva.

Not long after the publication of *Mr Tod*, Beatrix answered a letter from a six-year-old who asked her what really did happen to Tommy Brock and Mr Tod. 'I am sorry to tell you they are still quarrelling. Mr Tod has been living in the willow till he was flooded out; at present he is in the stick house with a bad cold in his head. As for the end of the fight – Mr Tod had nearly half his hair pulled out of his brush (= tail) and five bad bites, especially one ear, which is scrumpled up (like you sometimes see nasty old Tom Cat's ears). The only misfortune to Tommy Brock – he had his jacket torn and lost one of his boots. So for a long time he went about with one of his feet bundled up in dirty rags, like an old beggar man. Then he found the boot in the quarry. There was a beetle in the boot and several slugs. Tommy Brock ate them. He is a nasty person. He will go on living in Mr Tod's comfortable house till spring time – then he will move off into the woods and live out of doors – and Mr Tod will come back very cautiously – and there will need to be a big spring cleaning!'

Beatrix had taken a long time to finish *Mr Tod* because of her involvement in another campaign. 'There is a beastly fly-swimming spluttering aeroplane careering up and down over Windermere; it makes a noise like ten million blue-bottles. It is an irritating noise here, a mile off, it must be horrible in Bowness. It seemed to be flying very well; but I am sorry it has succeeded. If others are built – or indeed this one – will very much spoil the Lake. It has been buzzing up and down for hours today and it has already caused a horse to bolt and smashed a tradesman's cart.' Her protests about the hydroplanes continued throughout the winter, and Beatrix wrote a long and colourful letter to *Country Life* drawing readers' attention to the danger of planes on Windermere and to the rumour that an aeroplane factory was to be built

(*above left*) A preliminary drawing for *The Tale of Mr Tod*. The published illustration (*above right*) shows Mr Bouncer and Tommy Brock now sitting in armchairs to smoke their pipe and cabbage leaf cigar.

In 1912 Beatrix waged a campaign against the noise and danger of flying boats on Windermere.

between Bowness Bay and the Ferry Nab. 'Everyone uses the ferry. On calm summer waters no voyage is more cheerful and pleasant than this crossing of Windermere. Those who live to the west can tell another tale of winter nights, when the ferry cannot cross in the teeth of the wind. Then the homecoming carriers are storm-stayed at Bowness, and the Crier of Claife calls in vain for the ferry-man. For the most part we accept these interruptions as a dispensation of Providence – and the climate . . . Our peaceful lake is disturbed by the presence of a hydroplane . . . Horses upon land may possibly become accustomed to it, but it is doubtful whether they will ever stand quietly as it swoops over their heads while on the boat. If they back while on the water, there will be an accident . . . It seems deplorable that this beautiful lake should be turned into another Brooklands or Hendon . . . A more inappropriate place for experimenting with flying machines could scarcely be chosen.'

Her letter was supported by the editor: 'Admiration [for the aeroplane] cannot prevent us from sympathising with the protest made by Mrs Potter . . .' and he added that he hoped perhaps aeroplanes would become quieter one day, as motor cars have: 'today two friends may sit in a motor and converse in a tone as low as they would use in an office or a drawing-room.'

In another letter to a friend Beatrix wrote, 'About the flying machine. It has been being built in a large shed half-way down towards the lower end of the Lake. Another was built some time ago at one of the boat builders yards in Bowness. The Bowness gentleman falls in every time he tries, it must be awfully cold in this weather!'

Beatrix drew up a petition against the flying machines and set about collecting signatures, approaching publishers because they would know the name 'Beatrix Potter' and farmers because they would support 'H. B. Potter *farmer*'. 'I think the most striking list is thirty-four doctors and nurses at the London Hospital, of whom thirty-one have visited the Lakes, collected by a nurse who had been to Sawrey.' The aeroplane factory was not built and before the year was out the planes had left Windermere.

Beatrix was spending more and more time in Sawrey. In 1909 she had bought a new farm there, Castle Farm, which had a small house facing Hill Top and affording a grand view of her land. She engaged a housekeeper, Mrs Rogerson, to look after the cottage, and she started to take an active part in local affairs, sitting on a committee concerned with preserving footpaths and judging trussed poultry at local shows. She also kept a close eye on all that went on at both farms. 'Quantities of lambs – nearly all twins. But the pig has only six pink cherubs ... a rat has taken *ten*

'I am much amused with 6 little ducks waddling about the garden ... They rush for presents of worms and caterpillars.'

On 13 July 1912 Rupert Potter photographed his daughter's second farm in Sawrey, Castle Cottage, which she had bought in 1909.

Beatrix's lawyer, William Heelis (with pipe and bowler), in an early family photograph. His parents are on his left.

fine turkey eggs last night. The silly hen was sitting calmly on nothing, Mr S. Whiskers having tunnelled underneath the coop, and removed the eggs down the hole! ... We have a very handsome bull that was bred here, but being all short people we think "Billy" will soon be too big for us to manage.'

Beatrix was now the owner of a considerable amount of land in and around Sawrey. In all her property dealings she had taken the advice of a local firm of solicitors, W. H. Heelis and Son of Ambleside and Hawkshead, an old-established firm well used to the transfer of Lake District property. She was looked after there by William Heelis, a good-looking man in his early forties, tall and

PLATE XXI (below) This gentleman mouse is a close relation of the one that appeared in *The Tailor of Gloucester*, 1902.

PLATE XXII (right) 'She tipped up the milk jug – that greedy old Cat!' From the folding panorama *The Sly Old Cat*, March 1906.

PLATE XXIII (right) 'Suddenly round a corner she met Babbitty Bumble.' From the manuscript of *Mrs Tittlemouse*, January 1910.

PLATE XXIV A background watercolour sketch for
the interior of the shop in *Ginger and Pickles*, 1909.

PLATE XXV 'Twice he put his pencil in his mouth,
and once he dipped it in the treacle.'

William Heelis in the garden of Battlebarrow House, Appleby, to which his mother moved when she was widowed in 1893. With him are (sitting left) his aunt Mrs Stampa, whose son was G. L. Stampa the *Punch* artist, (right) his sister Marion (May), and (foreground) his sister-in-law Sybil, wife of his brother George.

slim, the youngest of a family of three girls followed by eight boys. The first Heelis to 'come over' the Pennines from Yorkshire was Thomas Heelis in 1720, who went to Appleby as land agent to Lord Thanet, and for generations the Heelis family had been either land agents, doctors, solicitors or in the church. William Heelis's father was Rector of Kirkby Thore until his death in 1893, one of his brothers was Rector of Brougham and another Rector of Crosthwaite, and his brothers Alec and George were, like him, solicitors. William had been brought up in the rectory at Kirkby Thore, a few miles north of Appleby, and educated at Sedbergh where he had become a keen sportsman. He was now in partnership with his cousin, who was also a William Heelis. In order to distinguish between them, the Hawkshead locals had given them nicknames, 'Appleby Billie or Willie' for our William and 'Hawkshead Willie' for his cousin.

William Heelis had been very helpful to Beatrix in her acquisitions, keeping her informed of land coming on to the market,

The village of Near Sawrey photographed on a June day in 1985.

even attending sales on her behalf and then looking after the ensuing contracts and formalities. Although her father was a specialist in land conveyancing, Beatrix could hardly call upon her father's help when her parents had shown such disapproval of the whole business. From Mr Heelis she had had kindness and efficient and understanding support. He, in turn, admired this London woman's strength of character and her obvious pleasure in the countryside where he had been born and brought up. They had spent many hours together, planning extensions to her cottages and improvements to her land. Towards the end of 1912 William asked Beatrix to be his wife. Beatrix had grown very fond of Willie and there was no doubt in her mind about wanting to marry him, but once again she had her parents' wishes to consider – and their disapproval to face. Heelis certainly wasn't good enough for a Potter daughter. Rupert was eighty, his wife only seven years younger, and who would look after them if she got married?

Beatrix was showing signs of the strains of the past few years and during the winter she became ill, a serious illness that lasted well into the spring of 1913 and affected her heart again. Even her letters had to be written for her. 'I have been resting on my back for a week as my heart has been rather disturbed by the Influenza. I am assured it will recover with quiet.' By March she was getting better: 'The doctor has just been and he is so much pleased with

The main street of Near Sawrey as recorded by Rupert Potter's camera in May 1913.

my progress that I am going to keep flat for a few days longer. My heart now feels quite comfortable,' and by April she was back in Sawrey and gathering strength. 'I seem to get on very slowly, I am decidedly stronger and look perfectly well, but I was completely stopped by a short hill on trying to walk to the next village this afternoon. I believe persevering slow exercise is the best cure, I do not think there is anything wrong with my heart now.' She needed all her strength to overcome her parents' objections to her marriage; although she was nearly forty-seven years old, Beatrix was still reluctant to go against their wishes.

In 1913 Beatrix and her parents spent the summer at Lindeth How in Windermere. Rupert Potter had been seriously ill but returned to London so much recovered that his wife felt it time to dispense with his nurse altogether. Beatrix could see that they might soon be relying on her again. 'He is so well I am in fear they may not get anybody. If we were not coming to a difficult change amongst the house servants – I might be tempted to bolt at once, while he is well and cheerful! I was feeling the going away very much, but William has actually been invited up for a weekend soon – they never say much but they cannot dislike him.'

Help for Beatrix came from an unexpected direction, from Bertram, for it was now that he chose to tell his parents of his marriage to Mary seven years before. Helen and Rupert Potter's

131

Following her engagement to William Heelis, Beatrix became seriously ill. During her long recuperation she worked on 'a pig story'.

opposition to their daughter's marriage began to crumble as her determination grew, and eventually they gave their consent. The Warne family showed their understanding through Millie, who assured Beatrix that Norman would have approved.

There was much to be done before the wedding, which was planned for October. Beatrix and Willie had chosen Castle Cottage as their home and a large room was being built on to the side of the house. Beatrix also had a book to finish, for on the strength of her earlier promise, Warne had announced publication. 'I am all right now but it might have been wiser to give up the book, before they took orders for it.' Beatrix had been sketching

A black piglet rejected by John Cannon for Hill Top became Beatrix's pet – and the lovely Pig-wig in *Pigling Bland*.

pigs for use in a book for years and she had been working on a story during her long illness, but it was not until April 1913 that she had finally finished the text for *The Tale of Pigling Bland* and sent it to Harold, 'I enclose the pig story. *I* think is rather pretty.'

Beatrix had called on her farming experience for the new book, remembering an occasion when she went to collect some pigs for John Cannon. He was very particular about the pigs he bought, always insisting on ones with a pedigree and on this day the litter included a tiny black girl-pig which was naturally excluded from the sale. Beatrix however insisted on buying it, and when John Cannon refused to keep it anywhere near the others, Beatrix took it into the house. It slept in a basket by her bed and she bottle-fed it until it was old enough to look after itself. It became, of course, the 'perfectly lovely little black Berkshire pig', Pig-wig, who 'crossed the bridge hand in hand – then over the hills and far away she danced with Pigling Bland.'

The Tale of Pigling Bland was published in October 1913, the month that Beatrix Potter married William Heelis.

Beatrix forgot to put the peppermint into this picture of Pig-wig sitting in the firelight.

The book was to be produced in the same way as *Mr Tod*, with fewer colour plates and more black-and-white illustrations than the earlier ones, and that meant a great deal of last-minute drawing 'to fill the spaces', but it was finished at last and ready for publication just in time for the wedding. The book had been done under great pressure and in the copy that Beatrix dedicated to Willie she confessed, 'Peppermint accidentally omitted from p 67'. With another copy sent to a friend she wrote, 'I'm afraid it was done in an awful hurry and scramble. The portrait of two pigs arm in arm – looking at the sunrise – is not a portrait of me and Mr Heelis, though it is a view of where we used to walk on Sunday afternoons! When I want to put William into a book – it will have to be some very tall thin animal.'

Beatrix Potter and William Heelis were married in London on 14 October 1913, at St Mary Abbot's in Kensington. Beatrix Moore recalls that they came to see them in Wandsworth while they were on their honeymoon. 'I was about ten and it was the last time I remember seeing her, as she went up north after that. We always loved it when Beatrix came to see us. She used to arrive in her carriage, with a straw bonnet tied under her chin and carrying a cage of white mice which she let loose in the drawing room. She gave my sister, Hilda, and me party frocks which she had bought from Woollands. I remember mine well – it had beading on it and pink and blue ribbons. This time, when she and Willie came to see us, there was much laughter because she was "meeting a bull at the station". I presume it was something to do with the farm. After she went to live in the Lake District, she sent us a huge turkey every Christmas; I can see it now hanging from a nail in the cellar. Mother and Father used to have to pluck it and draw it.'

The first few months of the Heelis marriage were somewhat unsettled, partly because Castle Cottage was not yet ready, and partly because an old aunt of Willie's was ill in Appleby and needed to be visited regularly. In addition Warne were already asking for another book and although Beatrix had an idea for one there was just not enough time. 'I have inhabited three houses since marriage and have been having altogether too much to attend to at once.' Her father was seriously ill, and when cancer was diagnosed Beatrix returned to London to supervise his nursing. 'I found my father a little weaker after my absence of ten days, and he seems to have taken another step downhill these last two days. I shall be more free when we get a second nurse, but I don't like to make an apptmnt as I shall go back to Sawrey for a few days whenever there is a chance. He may last a good while, but it is scarcely to be wished.' She made eight journeys to London from Sawrey in the first four months of 1914, worrying about her father and calming down her mother. Willie remained in Sawrey, joining Beatrix

Beatrix and Willie on their wedding day, 14 October 1913. They were photographed by Rupert Potter, who died only seven months later.

only when Rupert Potter died on the evening of 8 May. 'It has been a rather ghastly illness. We are very thankful it is over, as we feared he might drag on for weeks longer – he went suddenly in the end ... Mr Heelis is coming tonight and we are going to an hotel across the road as that really will be the most rest.' Mrs Potter was not making it easy for her only daughter and her new son-in-law.

Beatrix now had the problem of what to do about her mother. She brought her to stay in Sawrey but she was alone too much and 'found it rather dull'. Eventually Beatrix engaged a companion for her and installed them both in a furnished house in the village where they were to spend the next four years. 'It is the best plan, and I tell William it is highly complimentary to *him* that these old ladies take refuge in the neighbourhood; but it does keep *me* on the trot. I have had rather a hard summer.' It was already too late for Beatrix to start on a new book in time for Christmas. It would be the first year that Frederick Warne would be without a new title by Beatrix Potter on their list since *Peter Rabbit* was published in 1902 – and it was to be another three years before there would be a new Beatrix Potter at all.

In August the country was plunged into the war that was to change the whole condition of a nation and to deprive the country for ever of almost a million of its young men. Some of Willie's nephews left at once for the war and Beatrix had news that Bertram had volunteered but, somewhat to her relief, had been refused on account of his frail health. As the weeks went by she became concerned about Harold's family. 'There have been sad losses amongst local officers ... I do hope your nephews are all alive and unhurt – or not badly. Sometimes it is a relief to have them safe in hospital ... It is a weary job. A whole family of distant cousins went down in the Lusitania, father, mother, six children and nurse ... I am awfully sorry to hear about Bobbie Pearce, he seemed such a promising fine lad; and like your own son. It always seems as if the best are taken.'

Beatrix's life with Willie was taking on a pattern that was to continue for many years, Beatrix supervising the farming and keeping an eye on her mother and Willie working from his solicitor's office in Hawkshead. The war did not help in the smooth running of the farms: 'I feel nervous about the horses which are down on the police list, but at a pinch we can use cattle ... The ploughman got his calling up, in the very middle of ploughing. I'm afraid I am not in a particularly good temper.' It was the weather, however, that Beatrix was discovering to be the farmer's continuing

'A whole family of distant cousins went down in the Lusitania, father, mother, six children and nurse,' wrote Beatrix soon after the boat was torpedoed on 7 May 1915.

enemy, 'We have had a wild day here, storms of sleet, and all day wet lambs before the fire – the third dead since breakfast has just expired! There is not an atom of grass and the hill flocks must be in a pitiable state.' Later in the year it was the harvest that suffered, 'I am very worried with the corn, it is a sickening job, all grown together with sprouting and rotten straw. We have had *one* really sunny day since middle of August – I *never* remember such weather.' Her faithful old collie, Kep, died that year, too, and although she was a realist about the progress of time and, as a farmer, used to the death of animals, Kep had been with her for a long time and she had grown extraordinarily fond of him. She missed him badly but his place was eventually taken in her affections by 'a black and white bobtail, she is called ''Fleet''''.

Beatrix was becoming extremely concerned about the continuing inefficiency at Frederick Warne. Something was certainly wrong and it appeared to stem from Harold. 'I don't like going on indefinitely without some sort of accounts, you did not send any statement, as you talked of doing, after the New Year. The last I can lay my hand on is for 1911!! I think I have had one since then; but not for a long time. I am a healthy person, but think what it would look like for unbusiness if I happened to wind up. If it has got beyond keeping account of, it would be better to say so.'

Her letter brought reassurances from Harold that all was well but that the war was restricting the flow of money and making it difficult to keep up with the various routines of office life. Six months later Beatrix had still not received any money. Some years before, she had made an arrangement whereby, in the event of her death, the copyrights in her books should remain with the company. Now she might have to think again. Perhaps an approach to Fruing Warne would bring a better response? 'I promised not to ask the firm for payments while times were so difficult; but I think you will allow that the failure to send any statements at all is a trial of patience; the overlapping and unpunctuality had begun *long before the war* ... If the matter of accounts is not gone into satisfactorily by the end of January, I shall have to take some steps about it – not in an unfriendly spirit – but to put the matter on a more businesslike footing. For one thing I should instruct my London solicitors to alter my will; I cannot leave this muddle to go on accumulating. I am writing this without any consultation with my husband; for reasons which you may guess I feel a repugnancy to his intervening in any business between me and your family.'

Her approach to Fruing worked and the money was forthcoming, but Beatrix's confidence had been shaken and when, in June 1916, Harold Warne wrote for her permission to raise the price of the little books from 1/- to 1/3, she decided to take the opportunity to alter the wording of her contracts with Warne. 'I do not like the indefinite term of assignment to F.W. & Co their heirs and assigns – in view of the uncertain future for all trade . . . It is unthinkable that I should ever quarrel with you and your family but if there were ever a reconstruction of your business in the uncertain future I think I ought not to be in that indefinitely tied up position, in view of my easyness in the past.'

Beatrix's fears were well founded. In April 1917 Harold was arrested as he was walking down the street in Covent Garden with Fruing. Harold Edmund Warne, 56, publisher, was initially charged before the Lord Mayor in the Mansion House with 'uttering a bill of exchange for £988.10s.3d. knowing it to be forged'. He was not granted bail.

When old Mrs Warne died she had left to her eldest son the family fishing business in Jersey, a business that Harold had allowed to get into serious financial difficulties. The forged bill named in the charge had been drawn in the name of Messrs. William Fruing and Co. (Limited) of Jersey, as had other bills to the value of £13,623; the money meant for publishing was going to support fishing. On 27 April 1917 Harold Warne was sentenced to eighteen months' imprisonment for £20,000 forgeries. He was never to return to publishing. In court the defence was given leave to make a statement. 'The prisoner's brother was in no way implicated in the forgeries and knew nothing whatever about the matter.'

It was the prisoner's brother, Fruing, who now found himself in charge of a family publishing company that was fast approaching bankruptcy but with a most valuable asset in the published books and any future work of Beatrix Potter. The first thing Fruing had to do was to raise enough money to stop the company's debtors

Beatrix was becoming increasingly uneasy about Warne's finances, and *The Times* of 27 April 1917 showed that her fears were justified.

£20,000 BILL FORGERIES.

At the Central Criminal Court yesterday, before the Recorder, HAROLD EDMUND WARNE, 56, publisher, was sentenced to 18 months' imprisonment with hard labour on a charge, to which he pleaded "Guilty," of forging and uttering an acceptance to a bill of exchange for £985 14s. and the acceptance to another bill.

Mr. TRAVERS HUMPHREYS, for the prosecution, said the total amount the prisoner had obtained by means of forgeries was £13,623.

Mr. HUNTLY JENKINS, appearing for the defence, said that in addition to the bills mentioned by Mr. Travers Humphreys the prisoner wished it to be stated that he had uttered seven other bills of exchange, amounting to £6,495.

Mr. Huntly Jenkins said he wished to state that the prisoner's brother was in no way implicated in the forgeries and knew nothing whatever about the matter.

Witnesses were called on behalf of the prisoner and stated that he bore the highest reputation.

The Fruing Warnes' nanny
(here with Winifred and Eveline
in 1903) agreed to stay on with
the impoverished family
without wages.

foreclosing and that meant selling everything, the personal possessions of the immediate family and even his own watch and signet
ring. At the sale, members of the Warne staff bought back the
watch and ring and returned them to Fruing as a mark of their support – but they could hardly afford to buy back his house. Nearly
seventy years later Fruing's daughter, Winifred, remembers those
dark days very clearly. 'It all came as a dreadful shock to us. My
mother knew that the business wasn't doing well but she had no
idea it was so serious. My father had always been on the book side
rather than the money side and it came as an equal shock to him to
discover that his brother had been using the company's money to
save his own business. I remember my mother coming up to our
room to tell us that we would have to leave our lovely home in
Surbiton and she had to ask our nanny if she would stay on without wages. We went to a tiny house near Richmond Park and we
children hated it.'

(*above left*) 'Appley Dapply
Goes to the Cupboard'. An
1891 water-colour which was
reworked for inclusion in
*Appley Dapply's Nursery
Rhymes*, published for
Christmas 1917.

(*above right*) A rough design
for a page in an earlier version
of the book, discouraged by
Norman Warne in 1905.

In spite of her earlier misgivings and frustrations Beatrix was
sympathetic and eager to help, and Fruing asked her if she could
look after Winifred's dolls' house, the one that had been made by
Norman and used as the model for *Two Bad Mice*. 'Yes certainly I
will keep the poor Doll house for you, if you can manage to get it
packed and sent off. I wish I knew anywhere in London to store it;
but I don't like suggesting it to my mother, or writing to her caretakers at Bolton Gardens without her leave and knowledge. I don't
think she ever noticed that horrid report in *The Times*, and one
doesn't want to start anyone asking questions gratuitously. The
only other way I can think of, if you find the house too awkward to
pack, would be to try to lend it to a children's hospital, which
would be a kind and useful resting place. I am very glad Millie has
had the good luck to let her house, and without a regular sale. It *is*
dreadfully sad for you and Mary. I do feel sorry for you. But when
she gets over the wrench of leaving a pretty home, there will be less
housekeeping in a smaller house.'

The next request Fruing made of Beatrix was for her continued
involvement while the company was being restructured, and to
this she readily agreed, suggesting that Warne publish *Appley
Dapply's Nursery Rhymes* for Christmas. 'I hope Appley Dap will
be in time to be useful, and that it will be as good a season as can
be had during this war.' The original *Appley Dapply* had been in
the making since 1902 and was one of the books Beatrix had

A water-colour of the Amiable Guinea-pig not used in the published edition of *Appley Dapply's Nursery Rhymes.*

discussed with Norman. It was a collection of traditional and original rhymes that Beatrix had added to over the years and from which she now selected seven, with their illustrations, to make a little book to fit the series. 'I'm afraid this sounds very lazy, but you don't know what a scramble I live in; and the old drawings are some of them better than any I could do now.' The new book turned out well – 'I am much pleased with A. D. it makes a pretty little book,' and *Appley Dapply's Nursery Rhymes* was published in October 1917. Together with two new painting books, made from the old *Peter Rabbit Painting Book*, it gave strong Potter support to the battered company of Frederick Warne. The re-structuring had begun.

In May 1919 a new company was registered, Frederick Warne & Company Limited, and at the first board meeting Fruing Warne was elected managing director. For Fruing's children it was an exciting day. 'We were sent to bed early, before Daddy came back from the meeting, so we were out of the way. Our mother knew that we would be up at the crack of dawn the next morning and that they wouldn't want to be disturbed so she arranged to put a notice on the wardrobe on the landing telling us how the meeting went. When we came down there it was – "Daddy made Managing Director. £500 a year". It was wonderful.'

Beatrix had been consulted about the new company at every stage, for she was the largest creditor and it was important to have

The Town Mouse and the Country Mouse

'The Town Mouse and the Country Mouse', a water-colour by Beatrix for the Aesop fable that she retold as *Johnny Town-mouse*.

her agreement that the firm should continue in business. She was reluctant to spend any more time in London than was absolutely necessary and she sent her solicitor to meetings on her behalf. 'He will represent me, and strongly favour carrying on, and make a suggestion as to my share of indebtedness which I hope will be helpful. Only I want to say that it must be clearly understood that "H" never meddles again. I bear him no grudge, but I know and remember what a trial he has been, even to me, for many years.' Beatrix agreed that part of Warne's indebtedness to her should be paid in allotted shares, a move that tied her even more closely to the new company.

1918 had been another difficult year for her. The war was still dragging on and Willie had received his call-up papers but, as in her brother's case, his health was found to be Grade 3 which meant that he did not have to go. Then one day in June Beatrix was stunned to receive the news that Bertram had died of a cerebral haemorrhage while working in his garden in Ancrum. He was only forty-six but his years of drinking had taken their toll. When Beatrix went to Scotland for the funeral she found that, as usual, everyone was relying on her: 'What with the shock, the difficulty of getting to the funeral and back, and the number of letters I have had to write, since neither his widow nor my mother seemed able to write them – I am only just getting straight.' Beatrix had always been close to her brother; they had shared their love of painting and their fascination with animals; they had fought and won

(*above left*) Beatrix sketched an arch and a house in nearby Hawkshead for use in her picture of the cart arriving in town in *Johnny Town-mouse* (*above right*).

battles against parental disapproval. Although they had seen each other rarely since they had married and become farmers, Beatrix knew that she would miss Bertram badly, and in her sorrow she wrote to Hardwicke Rawnsley, 'I don't think I yet realise that Bertram is gone – in his prime, and in his usefulness. He had such a fine farm; and although his nature – sensitive and like his father's – and patriotic & upright to a rare degree – made him feel the war very keenly – I do think he found true happiness in hard useful manual work. It is good to remember how much more cheerful & contented he had seemed towards the last. He had not painted lately, but he hoped & intended to take it up again "after the war". He is buried like the Grasmere folks in the bend of a stream – a flowery graveyard with a ruined ivy-grown church and graves of the covenanters on the banks of Ale Water.'

Beatrix had also been working on a new book during the year. At first she had suggested a second nursery rhyme collection but Fruing asked for a story this time, if possible, and Beatrix searched through her various papers. 'Do you think this mouse story would do? It makes pretty pictures, but not an indefinite number as there is not a great deal of variety. A few years ago I amused myself by writing out several of Aesop's fables, this is one that got rather longer than the others.' It was the fable of the town mouse and the country mouse and the title of Beatrix's version was changed three times before she finally settled on *The Tale of Johnny Town-mouse*. Her work on the pictures had to be fitted in between the

In 1919 Beatrix bought Lindeth
How in Storrs, Windermere, for
her eighty-year-old mother.
Three of the four maids, the
two gardeners and the
chauffeur were photographed
by the 'tween maid.

more pressing demands of the farm. 'I have just come in after a
rough two hours' search for some sheep and lambs with a boy –
the old man being poorly. We got them; so that is done with ...
Somehow when one is up to the eyes in work with real animals it
makes one despise paper-book-animals.' *Johnny Town-mouse*
was set locally near Hill Top, with Hawkshead as the town and
the gardens of Sawrey as the country. Beatrix based her hero on
the local doctor, with whom Willie regularly played golf, even
including his bag of golf clubs in the cover picture, and she just
finished everything in time for Warne to get the book into the
shops for Christmas. She received her author's copies on the last
day of the war. In the notice of the book in *The Bookman* the
reviewer wrote, 'The pictures are among the very best Miss Potter
has done ... Miss Potter need not worry about rivals. She has
none. *Johnny Town-mouse* does even so accomplished an artist
and writer as herself much credit.'

Beatrix had lost none of her magic. She was, though, once again
faced with the problem of her mother. Throughout the war the
family house in Bolton Gardens had been inhabited only by a care-
taker, and Mrs Potter was reluctant to return to a lonely existence
there. By great good fortune, Lindeth How, the house where
Beatrix and her parents had spent the last few months before her
marriage to Willie, was on the market, and Beatrix bought it for
her mother. It was a fine, gabled stone Lakeland house, built in
Storrs, Windermere, in the late 1870s by a wealthy mill-owner. It
had a fine view over the lake – importantly on the opposite side to
Sawrey – and eighty-year-old Mrs Potter settled in there, with four
maids, two gardeners and the coachman-turned-chauffeur. Beatrix
brought some of the furniture up from London, and Mrs Potter
quickly resumed her old routine of sewing and visiting.

The Country Mouse
and
the Town Mouse.

PLATE XXVI Inscribed: 'The Country Mouse and the Town Mouse'.
Johnny Town-mouse was published in 1918.

PLATE XXVII Four of the dinner cards made by Beatrix for use at Melford Hall in Suffolk, the home of her cousin.

PLATE XXVIII One of a set of twelve table mats based on *Jemima Puddle-duck*. Here Mrs Cannon feeds the poultry.

Beatrix Potter. 1929

Dance of the Leaf fairies – invented after seeing th Folk dancing festival at Underley.

Life for the Heelises in Sawrey was busy but it was also fun. Willie was an enthusiastic country dancer and often went off on his Bradbury motorcycle to dance in the neighbouring village. Now and then Beatrix went along too in her pony and trap, but only to watch. She was enchanted by the local country and folk dancing and with all that went with it. 'The stone-floored farm kitchen where first we danced "The Boatman" and heard the swinging lilt of "Black Nag". The loft with two fiddles where country dancers paced "The Triumph", three in arm under the arched hands. The long drive home in frosty starlight with a load of rosy sleepy village girls wrapped up in rugs. Coniston, and the mad barbaric music of the Kirkby-Mazzard Sword Dance, when a beheaded corpse springs up and holds a wheel of wooden swords aloft. Chapel Stile in Langdale where we came out into deep snow from a dance over the store. "Haste to the Wedding", "Pop Goes the Weasel" and "We Won't Go Home Until Morning!" The Morris bells and baldricks! The plum cake and laughter. Fat and thin, and high and low, the nimble and the laggard, the toddler and the grey-haired gran – all dancing with a will.'

As well as playing golf whenever he could, Willie was a keen bowler and regularly won tournaments at the local club, and there was nothing he liked better than a good day's shooting. Together Beatrix and Willie went to Heelis family parties, for which Willie had for once to change from the favourite knickerbockers into a

Willie Heelis was an enthusiastic country dancer and Beatrix often went along to watch the dancing – and to draw.

Willie was a keen sportsman and he won a number of bowling cups in local tournaments.

proper suit and Beatrix had to leave her clogs at home. One story about them preparing for a party with their cousins, the Gaddums, has been handed down in the family. 'As a result of the rheumatic fever she had as a young woman, B was left with a bare patch on the top of her head, which is why she always wore a hat. For this particular occasion she decided that she might try wearing a hair-piece instead but neither of her sisters-in-law could lend her one, having too good heads of hair of their own to need them. Then B thought of her father's old barrister's wig – until she remembered that it had two pigtails on it! In the end she sat down and made a

The local Pace Eggers, the Jolly Boys, were photographed by Beatrix in 1912 performing their play at Easter-time.

Every Easter Beatrix decorated pace eggs for the children of Sawrey to use in their egg races.

lace cap which afterwards she often wore when she went out and which she wore nearly all the time when she was an old lady.'

Beatrix and Willie were generous in their support of the local activities of Sawrey and the surrounding area. They would lend a field for the celebration of a coronation or a jubilee, they bought the dresses for the local team of folk dancers, and they always gave a warm welcome to the carollers at Christmas and to the Pace Eggers when they came at Easter. In 1919 Beatrix helped to set up a nursing trust in the area, endowing the charity which provided a district nurse for the parishes of Sawrey, Hawkshead and Wray

until the National Health Service took over nearly thirty years later. An appeal for help to the Heelises was not often turned away, but the case had to be a good one. A request in 1920 for Beatrix to release land in Sawrey for a bowling green did not find much favour, in spite of Willie's prowess at the sport: 'I have never approved the taking of productive agricultural land for purposes of recreation ... A bowling green is always more or less derelict in winter; and a good many public recreation grounds become untidy and desolate when the novelty wears off.' One of the causes that did attract her sympathy was that of the Southern Irish Loyalists Relief Association. To them she made 'a kind gift of £3'.

Beatrix spent much of her time with her animals. 'I have cows and sheep and horses, and poultry. I look after the poultry and rabbits and pony and my own particular pet pig. She is called Sally; she follows me about the farm like a dog, through gates and along the road, and if she gets left behind, I call Sally! Sally! and she gallops. I am very fond of rabbits. I have big brown Belgian rabbits, and silver grey; and one rabbit is chocolate colour ... I seem able to tame any sort of animal.'

Although both Beatrix and Willie loved the Lake District deeply, there was a short time just after the war had ended when they seriously thought of leaving it for ever. They discussed the possibility of emigrating to Canada and they even got as far as choosing where they would settle – along the St Lawrence below Lake Ontario, but their bonds with the country they loved were too strong to break and they stayed in Sawrey.

Beatrix was being pressed hard by Warne for a new book but she realised that she no longer felt the urgency; her eyes were tired, her mother was being as difficult as ever and there were more pressing things in Sawrey that needed her attention. At the same time, she had promised to support the new company and she knew that they needed her help, so after her first suggestion of a new collection of nursery rhymes had met with a lack of enthusiasm, she selected another one of her Aesop retellings, *The Tale of Jenny Crow*, and sent it to London. The new managing director startled her by sending it back, saying 'It is not Miss Potter, it is Aesop' and that he would prefer instead an earlier story he had seen and liked about a pigeon, 'a very brilliant little manuscript'. Beatrix was not at all pleased, 'I do bar the namby pamby pigeons for this season! The backgrounds of Rye are attractive, but it is nothing but pigeons over and over as regards illustration ... You do not realise that I have become more – rather than less obstinate as I grow older; and that you have no lever to make use of with me; beyond sympathy with you and the old firm, nothing else would induce me to go on at all. You see I am not short of money. I never have cared tuppence either for popularity or for the modern child; they are

(opposite) Beatrix at the Woolpack Show, Eskdale, with Harry Lamb, who was Secretary of the Herdwick Sheepbreeders' Association and Editor of *Lamb's Shepherd Guide*. Beatrix is wearing tweeds woven from the wool of her Herdwick sheep and has her usual clogs on her feet.

Beatrix based another story on an Aesop fable, but *The Tale of the Birds and Mr Tod* was never published. Here Mr Tod gazes up at Melford Hall.

The Peter Rabbit 'side-shows', as Beatrix called them, were doing well and bringing in good royalties.

pampered and spoilt with too many toys and books. And when you infer that my originality is more precious than old Aesop's, you *do* put your foot in it!'

Fruing Warne, alarmed by the tone of Beatrix's letter, hastily back-tracked and urged her to work on *Jenny Crow* after all, so they would have a new book for Christmas, but by August Beatrix had done only a few drawings. She was losing heart: 'I can see nothing after staring at them for a bit ... The whole thing is rather a mess! I am not willing to get stronger glasses after only one year's wear. The oculist said there was nothing wrong with my eyes, beyond 53 years of rather unmerciful usage. They will last my time, I hope; but you must *not* count on my going on doing books of coloured illustrations. Find someone else.'

The idea of facing a season without a new book by his star performer was almost too much for Fruing and he seized on Beatrix's suggestion that someone else might help her. There was in the Warne office a resident artist, Mr Stokoe, who had been called on in the past to touch up a pie-dish here or to strengthen a colour there, and he certainly would be available to help, but Beatrix was somewhat taken by surprise that Fruing had even considered her suggestion and hastened to reassure him that she would manage on her own after all. So Warne announced that *Jenny Crow*, or *The Tale of the Birds and Mr Tod* as it had now become, would be ready in time for Christmas and that the travellers should start taking orders.

However, by November there was still no sign of the rest of the drawings and Beatrix had to admit that she had not even started on them. 'It has not been through idleness! It is absolutely hopeless and impossible to finish books in summer.' It was not as if Warne had not got what Beatrix called 'the side-shows' on which to concentrate their sales efforts that year, the Peter Rabbit game and the calendars, though she knew that the Peter Rabbit slippers were sold out. 'I am glad you are having a good season – apart from my misdeeds – which you will have to put up with sooner or later – for you don't suppose I shall be able to continue these d...d little books when I am dead and buried!! I am utterly tired of doing them, and my eyes are wearing out. I will try to do you one or two more for the good of the old firm; but it is quite time I had rest from them – especially as there is still other work that I should like to finish for my own pleasure. I remain with kind regards and very moderate apologies yours sincerely Beatrix Heelis.'

Beatrix did not give up drawing altogether but there was no new book the following year or the one after that. 'I think it only honest to tell you that book is not getting on yet. The country is looking beautiful enough to give me inspiration; but I seem as if I can't screw it out, and my eyes are always tired ... I will have

In May 1920 Beatrix's dear
friend Canon Hardwicke
Rawnsley died. They were
photographed together in
Windermere in 1912.

to rummage in my portfolios. But they only cause me wonder,
how I ever drew so much and so well, while I could see.'

In May 1920 Beatrix's dear friend Canon Hardwicke Rawnsley
had died and been buried in Crosthwaite churchyard. Beatrix was
missing him badly, for she had known this generous and wise man
for much of her life. She had been greatly influenced by him, and it
was he who taught her that it was sometimes necessary to fight to
safeguard the natural beauty of the countryside and to preserve the
traditions and skills of the people who lived there. It was Hardwicke Rawnsley who had first encouraged her to seek publication
for *Peter Rabbit*, and over the years he had become deeply devoted
to Beatrix. When his first wife died Beatrix had been married to
Willie for two years and Hardwicke married another old friend,
but there is strongly held opinion in the Rawnsley family today
that 'the love of his life was Beatrix'.

In the absence of a new book from Miss Potter, Warne were
planning to publish *Peter Rabbit* and *Benjamin Bunny* in French.

The 'new' Potter books for 1921 were *Benjamin Bunny* and *Peter Rabbit* in French.

The idea had first been mooted as long ago as 1907, when German versions had also been discussed, but it was not until 1912 that full and careful translations had been made by a French schoolteacher, Mlle Ballon, in co-operation with Beatrix, whose French was excellent and who wanted to ensure that none of the spirit and feeling of the books was lost. She was anxious that the French versions should be 'coloquial without being slangy ... Please. Do not try to keep so near the *English* words – it only spoils the *French*.' Flopsy, Mopsy and Cotton-tail became Flopsaut, Trotsaut and Queue-de-Coton and Benjamin Bunny became Jeannot Lapin but Mr Mac-Grégor acquired only an accent. Beatrix was happy with the result: 'I like the French translations, it is like reading some one else's work – refreshing.' Plans to publish *Pierre Lapin* and *Jeannot Lapin* in 1914 had been postponed when war became inevitable, but everything had been safely kept and even the type had remained set up, so production went ahead in 1921 and that year there were two 'new' books by Beatrix Potter on the Warne list.

Beatrix Potter's publishers were also at the time fighting off a flood of Peter Rabbit imitations and piracy. They took the Oxford University Press to task for publishing a pop-up version of *Peter Rabbit* without permission, though it was acknowledged that 'there is nothing particularly new in the idea of the Rabbit jumping up as the book opens, as this sort of thing was done thirty years ago by Deans and Tucks'. It was, however, a breach of copyright, and the book was withdrawn from sale and 1d a copy damages were paid for those already sold.

On Fruing's return from a visit to America he reported to Beatrix, 'Peter himself, from the various ways and manners in which he is being pirated and reproduced and made use of by American exploiters, is possibly the most popular juvenile character in literature, bar none.' This popularity of *Peter Rabbit* in America extended to Beatrix's other books, too, all of which had been safely protected, and Beatrix was receiving an increasing number of fan letters from children in America, as well as from Australia and New Zealand. One day in June 1921 she received a letter, not from a child, but from a librarian, the Superintendent of Children's Work in the New York Public Library. She was staying in Grasmere and had just ordered fifty copies each of *Pierre Lapin* and *Jeannot Lapin* for one of the French libraries she had been visiting, sponsored by the American Committee for Devastated France. In her letter Anne Carroll Moore told Beatrix of the work being done in France and asked if she could come over to Sawrey to tell her more. Beatrix was delighted and invited her to lunch; the lunch continued into tea and tea into staying the night, and the invitation was extended to Anne Carroll Moore's wooden doll, Nicholas Knickerbocker, from which she was never parted.

Leslie Brooke's portrait of Anne Carroll Moore, the eminent children's librarian from New York, who visited Beatrix in 1921.

Beatrix and her American visitor talked for hours, about books and about children, about painting and about the countryside, and Miss Moore was taken on a conducted tour of the farm. She was shown Beatrix's portfolio of drawings and consulted about whether or not a second nursery rhyme collection would be well received. The encounter was a great stimulus to Beatrix at a time when she was starting to feel that her book days might be over. Her work was certainly as popular as ever in terms of sales, but she received precious little public acknowledgement of their existence and books for children were looked upon as toys rather than as a serious contribution to literature. Unexpectedly, a woman highly qualified in the library field, with a status of which there was no equivalent in Britain, had arrived on her doorstep, full of praise and appreciation for all those years of hard work. Anne Carroll Moore's visit was just the tonic Beatrix needed; it was also the first of many similar pilgrimages by other Americans and of many close friendships that gave her much pleasure for the rest of her life.

As a direct result of her discussions with Miss Moore, Beatrix resumed work on *Cecily Parsley's Nursery Rhymes*, designing it as a companion volume to *Appley Dapply*. Choosing a further eight of the rhymes from her original collection, she worked on the drawings whenever she could steal time from her other distractions – 'I

Anne Carroll Moore persuaded Beatrix to work on a new book, *Cecily Parsley's Nursery Rhymes*, which was published for Christmas 1922. Warne insisted that the apples and cider (*above left*) should be changed to cowslips and cowslip wine (*above right*) for the published book.

would have got them done this week but I am plagued with visitors and poultry, and a bad drought' – and everything was finally finished just in time for Warne to put the book into production for Christmas 1922, in spite of a last-minute delay when Beatrix insisted on restoring to 'Three Blind Mice' the previously omitted line about cutting off their tails with a carving knife. Beatrix sent a special copy of *Cecily Parsley* to Anne Carroll Moore's doll, Nicholas, telling him it was a book 'for which you are partly responsible!' She did not dedicate the book to Nicholas, however. It is 'For little Peter of New Zealand', the nephew of one of her New Zealand fans, Bessie Hadfield. When Peter was orphaned at the age of two – his father was killed on the Somme, his mother a victim of influenza – his aunt 'tucked me onto the end of her family of four'. Little Peter grew up to be Dr R. P. Tuckey, a family doctor in Wellington.

chapter five

'We are getting lambs here, and should be in full swing on the sheep farms in another week.'

Beatrix with her favourite collie, Kep

IN THE SUMMER of 1922 Beatrix had arranged to rent a cottage which had once been part of the old Castle Cottage farmhouse to Miss Margaret Hammond, her governess's niece, who had helped her with her electioneering work in London. The cottage was let initially for just six months but in 1924 Miss 'Daisy' Hammond and her companion, Miss Cecily Mills, were still there – and they were to remain there, as close neighbours and friends, for many years to come. They looked after each other's dogs, they kept an eye on each other's gardens and they exchanged recipes and pots of jam.

For the next few years Beatrix turned all her energies towards farming, and in 1924 she bought one of the most spectacularly situated hill-farms in the Lake District, Troutbeck Park Farm, standing at the head of the Trout Beck Valley, near Windermere, its stone farmhouse sheltering beneath the rise of Troutbeck Tongue. It was a large farm of over 2,000 acres supporting many hundreds of sheep, the majority of them Beatrix's favourite Herdwicks, and its acquisition gave her an important place in Lake District farming. She was now a considerable property owner, with three farms in Sawrey and the newly acquired Troutbeck Park across the other side of Lake Windermere. She bought a car, a brand new Morris Cowley, and her mother's footman, Walter, came to drive it for her. As Beatrix made daily visits to her properties the car became a familiar sight making its stately way round the lake, but she was not the only one on the road. 'All the main roads through this district are being widened on account of the motors. There are such crowds of trippers in summer, and the char-a-bancs are very awkward on narrow country roads. Some people think it is spoiling the countryside, but there is no help, for everybody will have a small car or a motor byke presently.'

To look after the sheep on her new farm Beatrix was determined to find the best shepherd, and after a good deal of careful inquiry she found the man she was looking for, Tom Storey, who at the time was working on a big sheep farm in Kentmere. In 1985 Tom still recalled clearly the day she tracked him down. 'Saturday night it was, in November. We'd just finished milking and she came through the shippon door wearing clogs and with a car standing out on the road. She was quite smart for her age – a bonny-looking woman to tell you the truth. "Are you Tom Storey?" she said. "Yes," I said. "Well, I've come to see if you'll manage my sheep. I'll double your wages whatever you're getting now." Of course I agreed. "How old are you?" she asked. "I'm just thirty," I told her. "Well I'm double your age," she said. "I'm just sixty." So I went to Troutbeck Park. Although I was married with two children it was very lonely at the Park but I didn't mind. It was good sheep country and we did well. The farm was rotten with

(opposite) In 1924 Beatrix bought Troutbeck Park Farm, spectacularly situated at the head of the Trout Beck Valley. As her shepherd at Troutbeck Park Beatrix employed Tom Storey (inset), who lived in the village of Near Sawrey until his death in March 1986.

Beatrix was frequently annoyed
by newspapers attributing the
Peter Rabbit books to Beatrice
Webb (née Potter), seen here
with Sidney Webb in 1929.

In a letter to Warne Beatrix
suggested that she might be
photographed with a favourite
pig or cow to counteract the
photographs of the Webbs.

sheep fluke when she bought it; they used to die like flies. It were
lucky the fluke-worming pill came out at the time she bought the
farm. She was good like that; ask her to get anything for the sheep
and she'd do it right away. That next spring we lambed a thousand
sheep at the Park.'

Beatrix was becoming immersed in the all-absorbing life of the
sheep farmer but there were the occasional outside interruptions
which demanded her attention. For some time Warne had been
annoyed by continued newspaper reference to Beatrice Webb, Mrs
Sidney Webb, 'author of the famous *Peter Rabbit* books', an
understandable confusion as Beatrice Webb had been Beatrice
Potter (no relation) before her marriage. When, in yet another article, it was repeated, Beatrix took action herself. 'I enclose a copy of
a letter which I am posting to the Editor of the Sunday Herald . . . I
usually take no notice, as even the insult of being mistaken for Mrs
S. Webb is preferable to publicity. But if the Webbs are going to
become prominent along with our new rulers, the error had better
be contradicted; for I do not think that nice old-fashioned people
who like my books would like them quite so much if they believed
them to be of socialist origin . . . Mr Heelis is much edified by the
portraits of Mr and Mrs Webb on the front page of the Herald; he
says that it is adding insult to injury to suggest that Miss Beatrix
Potter is married "to such a little animal"! He thinks it wants stop-
ping. I should not like my real name to have to come out; if the
thing unfortunately spreads I think the best contradiction would
be to get photographed along with a favourite pig or cow and get it
inserted in some more genteel newspaper? I had lately a pig that

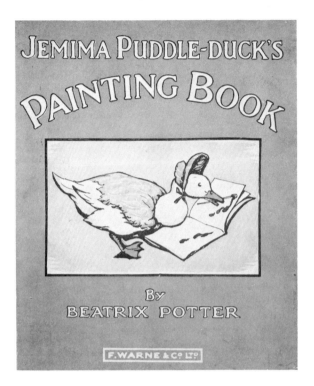

In 1925 Warne devised a second
painting book, this time
featuring Jemima Puddle-duck,
and Beatrix somewhat
reluctantly agreed to do the
pictures.

continually stood on its hindlegs leaning over the pig stye, but its
hanging up, unphotographed and cured now.'

Fruing Warne was again urging Beatrix to do a new book, or at
the very least to do a new painting book, and he sent her a plan for
The Jemima Puddle-duck Painting Book. Beatrix somewhat reluctantly agreed to work on it. 'I think I shall be able to do these
drawings easily with a quill pen; they are very much better than
the illustrations in my latest books. I understand your feeling from
the business point of view – but I doubt if I could ever explain *mine*
to you. You as publishers like the Peter Rabbit series, naturally
enough, and pressed me to go on with them after I was sick of
them – there are only about five I ever cared about. The clay-faced
paper and over-much-colour illustrated has always been against
my taste; but new line might sell less well, and is not encouraged
by you. I have always been too loyal to think of another publisher;
but sometimes when I get hold of other people's books I feel how
pleasant (and expensive) it would be to be privately printed just as
one liked without having to think of travellers and shops.' Beatrix
also told Fruing that she had been visited by a man who wanted
her to do a regular piece for the *Daily Graphic*. 'There arrived a
wandering taxi from Windermere containing the very image of
Johnny Town-mouse, walking stick, coat and all (except merci-
fully the bag) ... After half an hour's insinuating conversation he
wandered back, leaving me to "think it over".'

Fruing sensed danger and hurried up to Sawrey himself, with the
result that Beatrix rejected the advances of the newspaper and
agreed to think about another 'proper' book. It was to be about a

guinea pig. 'I have got a white guinea pig. I call him "Tuppeny", he is rather like a rat without a tail, he has the same kind of little pink hands and feet. He is a very talkative friendly person – only he *won't* let me touch him. He is in a small rabbit hutch with wire netting on the bottom and he nibbles the grass off short. Directly he hears my footstep he begins to twitter like a little bird, but if I try to touch him – he rushes about his box. Perhaps he will get tame in time.' Even Tuppeny did not do the trick, however, for Fruing's visit had depressed Beatrix deeply. 'I am afraid you will be vexed to hear that I have done nothing yet about another book. I scarcely know how to explain my feeling, it sounds so ungracious. I was in the mood to try something fresh, and I was afraid before you arrived that your visit would put me off it – and it did; by no fault of my visitor's. It brought back such a nightmare of painful memories.'

Her spirits were lifted though by the growing number of visitors from overseas, not only from America but from Australia, too, families with young children, librarians and teachers, all of them full of enthusiasm for the little books and all appreciative of the beautiful country in which Beatrix had chosen to make her home. Although she strongly discouraged any kind of personal publicity in the press and already had a reputation for being reclusive and even antagonistic to requests for biographical details or for visits

The fine old furniture at Hill Top was more often than not bought by Beatrix at local auctions and sales.

by British librarians, these visiting fans from overseas were assured of a warm welcome in Sawrey. 'I am always pleased to see Americans, I don't know what I think about you as a nation (with a big N!) but the individuals who have looked for Peter Rabbit have all been delightful.'

Beatrix received her visitors in Hill Top which was where she did all her drawing work and where she kept the things she valued most. Over the years she had collected pottery and china and she had some fine examples in cabinets there. She also collected furniture, about which she was very knowledgeable, visiting local sales and rescuing Chippendale and Sheraton chairs, fine court cupboards and oak chests from certain destruction. Hill Top was beginning to take on the air of a museum.

In Castle Cottage there were now three permanent residents, for Beatrix and Willie were looking after Willie's brother, Arthur, who was too ill to be left alone at Brougham Rectory any longer. He was an eccentric and difficult man and kept Beatrix on her toes. She wrote regularly to the rest of the family with news of his condition and she nursed him until he died in 1926. 'Our poor invalid Arthur Heelis has peacefully fallen asleep. It is a release for him and will be a relief when one gets used to it.' The relief took a long time to come, though, for six years later Beatrix commented in a letter, 'The death of one who has been ill for many months leaves a

Beatrix had a keen interest in china and pottery. These old Staffordshire figures were drawn by her when she was staying at Gwaynynog.

Mrs Rogerson was the housekeeper at Castle Cottage for many years. She was photographed in 1940 holding Middy, a descendant of Duchess from *The Pie and The Patty-pan*.

great gap ... I never thought how much I would miss him, when I missed his stick tapping on the bedroom floor.' Castle Cottage was not the easiest of houses in which to have an invalid, for the Heelises were averse to any form of modernisation. Their house-keeper, Mrs Rogerson, found it hard to get help. 'There was no electricity. Mrs Heelis would use a candle when she was writing before her husband came in for tea. Then the oil-lamps were turned on. I wasn't surprised that her eyes began to fail. She used to say that maids who weren't prepared to trim the lamps and keep them clean and wanted electric light instead could leave.'

Hill Top Farm had its usual complement of sheepdogs, and Beatrix's favourite at this time was Nip, 'a black and white bitch, a very good one. She was bred at Brothers' Water.' There were also Fly and Glen, and Meg, 'a meritorious, hardworking little dog'. Beatrix loved them all, but Nip was getting old and it was time to start training a new working dog. Beatrix chose a puppy from Nip's latest litter. 'I wish Fly to learn to work sheep. She must

The dogs at all the farms worked hard, and Beatrix usually had a favourite among them.

learn with *hens*. This is not as naughty as it looks, she never bites! When she has turned them she lies down. She sometimes puts them into the hen hut. Considering she is quite a baby – she is very promising. But she is frightened of sheep at present.'

In 1927 Beatrix asked Tom Storey if he would move from Troutbeck Park to Hill Top, to manage the farm and to breed and show her sheep. '"I'll give you another pound on your wage if you'll come to Sawrey," she said. So I went. She didn't know a lot about sheep then but she loved them, the Herdwicks. We worked well together. I used to take the milk in to her every morning and tell her the day's work plan. She very seldom asked me to change it. We won prizes for Herdwicks that very first year at Hawkshead Show and she was as pleased as a dog with two tails. I went to nearly every show with Mrs Heelis. We were unbeaten with ewes from 1930 until 1939. She won all sorts of prizes, like silver teapots and salvers and tankards – she used to give me all the tankards. We got on well and I stayed for twenty years, but then I knew her. If

Warne suggested that Beatrix might parallel Kate Greenaway's series of almanacs. This pencil drawing (*above left*) made at Bedwell Lodge in 1891 was the basis for the frontispiece of *Peter Rabbit's Almanac for 1929* (*above right*), the first and the last of the series.

you met Mrs Heelis with her head down you just walked past. If she had her head up you said, "Good morning".'

In the evenings Beatrix worked on some drawings for a new book. Warne had suggested that she imitate the successful Kate Greenaway Almanacs with a Beatrix Potter one, using some of the pictures she had been doing as greeting cards for her favourite charity, the Invalid Children's Aid Association, and they sent her the best-selling *Kate Greenaway Birthday Book* as an example to follow. Beatrix was extremely critical of it. 'I should imagine that Miss Greenaway was a very prolific designer and had most of these little figures in her portfolio, and pieced out the number with some [that] can only be called *rubbish*.' Hastily Fruing Warne concurred. 'We quite agree with your criticism of the K.G. drawings. Kate Greenaway could not draw, but she understood perhaps harmony of colour and was the first artist apparently to popularise the draping of children in something better than the hideous early Victorian garments that our mothers clothed us in – quite the correct mode of the time.' Beatrix decided that she would do some pictures specially rather than use old ones, and when Warne heard that they were all to be of rabbits they suggested changing the title of the new book to *Peter Rabbit's Almanac*. Beatrix found it hard work drawing in colour again. 'I cannot see to do them on dark days, and the lambing time is beginning, when it is not possible to neglect out of door affairs.'

The drawings were finished by the start of the summer of 1927, but Beatrix was not at all happy when the proofs of the *Almanac* arrived. 'Please let me know if this wretched sample is *final*? I know one thing; it is the first and the last.' Fruing Warne agreed that a certain amount of reworking was necessary and that would mean postponing publication until the end of the following year. Fruing did not live to see it, for he died in February 1928. He had been ill with pneumonia for some weeks but seemed to be recovering enough to go way for a recuperative holiday when he collapsed with a coronary heart attack. He was only sixty-six and his death came as a shock to everyone; the years of strain had taken their toll. For Beatrix it was the end of nearly thirty years of close friendship – and of successful business partnership – with the Warne family. Although Fruing had a son, he had not followed him into the family business and the new managing director was Fruing's brother-in-law, Arthur Stephens, a director of the firm for some time and the secretary of a paper company. For Beatrix it would be almost like starting again.

Meanwhile there was much to occupy her in Sawrey. For some years she had allowed Girl Guides to camp in her fields or, if it was very wet, in the farm buildings in Troutbeck, Hawkshead and Sawrey. She enjoyed having them there, even if sometimes they presented her with some unusual problems. 'They frequently inhabit my barn, but I have never received any rent; only an abomination called "slides", with which young persons do up their hair; but unwholesome for cows, when subsequently eating hay beds; they also left buttons and paper in the hay. The dairy maid had to pick it over being rewarded by the treasure trove, and was satisfied with her bargain.'

Beatrix helped the Guides when they needed help, lending her car and chauffeur to drive a suspected case of appendicitis home to Manchester or offering £10 towards the hiring of tents if it was shortage of money that was preventing the 1st Chorlton-cum-Hardy Company from their regular visits. 'It is always a pleasure to help Guides and it brings its own reward – for surely it is a blessing when old age is coming, to be able still to understand and share the joy of life that is being lived by the young. If *I* slept in a tent I might get sciatica; I enjoy watching Guides, smiling in the rain.' She liked to walk down to the camp in the late afternoons to see

"Peter Rabbit and the Guides at Troutbeck Park" from Beatrix Potter May 31st 1928

The Girl Guides camped regularly on Beatrix's land and she often joined in their activities and celebrations.

Joan Thornely, one Girl Guide
who camped in Sawrey in 1931,
still has her treasured
autograph book.

how they were faring and to join in their camp-fire tea parties and
sing-songs. She gave them autographed copies of her books as
prizes for competitions and even posed for photographs. 'I am
delighted to have the photographs, they are most successful and
the camp makes such a pretty picture. I can recognise many of the
Guides. We have a laugh at ME and I ought to have had my fine
new teeth in! I look a good natured old body at all events.'

Beatrix's mother had settled down well at Lindeth How and she
agreed that the time had come to sell 2 Bolton Gardens. Naturally
it was Beatrix who had to do all the work. 'I went to London for a
week (!) to clear my parents' house in South Kensington. My
mother had not lived there for 11 years; and there were the
accumulations of 60 odd years – perplexing, overwhelming, grimy
with London soot. I had no sentimental repinings as I had been dis-
contented and never strong as a young person in London – but
what a task! and what to keep and what to sell? with a rather
imperious old mother awaiting 3 van loads in Windermere. She
was asking for various articles to the end of her long life; I think
"caretakers" had taken toll – not me.'

Mrs Potter lived a comparatively isolated life in Lindeth How,
with her maids, her beloved dog, Betty, and the canaries which
she bred in cages round her bedroom. Every week she sent her
favourite maid, the cook Louisa Towers whom she always called
Lucissa, into Windermere in the chauffeur-driven car to buy an
apple for the birds. Lucissa (now Louisa Rhodes) has never forgot-
ten how embarrassed she was. 'I had to go to the vegetable shop
and ask for a penny apple and nothing more. At first I daren't go
but I had to go every week for a penny apple for the canaries.'

Beatrix rarely crossed the lake to see her mother and when she
did make the effort she was not always welcome. Mrs Rhodes remembers her visits well. 'Mrs Heelis wasn't very friendly towards
me. She used to ring up and Mrs Potter would say, "What does she
want?" She had abrupt manners, Mrs Potter, in her way – and I
heard her say, "But you can't have the car to meet you, it's
Lucissa's day for shopping." Mrs Heelis would walk all the way
from Sawrey down to the ferry and she was wanting the car to
meet her at this side, but Mrs Potter wouldn't let the car go for her
before it had taken me shopping for my penny apple. Beatrix used
to be raging. She had to walk up this side, too. I ask you, what
could I do? I was being loyal to the person that was paying my
wages and Mrs Heelis used to blame me, but I wasn't anxious to
go for a penny apple.

'They were both very strong willed, you know ... Knowing the
Beatrix Potter books, you really wouldn't think that she had it in
her to do those beautiful things. We never associated her with anything like that. All we associated her with were her clothes, or her

Sarah Jane ('Nana') and Jim
Patterson were the cook and
head gardener at Lindeth How
in 1919.

wellingtons, ragged clothes – and sheep. Once when she came in
from the ferry she said that she had met this tramp and he said to
her, "It's gay weather for the likes of thee and me, missus," and
she roared and laughed as she told us about it. But if you had seen
her; she had a pair of old wellingtons on, a mackintosh too big for
her and a sort of soft, floppy hat. She was like someone on the run.
Of course, when she spoke it was different. She couldn't be
bothered with people, all her interest was in the farm and the
cattle.'

Beatrix's visits to London were now very rare. She still had
friends there, the Woodwards and the Moores in particular, but
the Moore children were all grown up. Noel had become a priest
and was working in the East End of London, his brother Eric had
followed in father's footsteps and was a civil engineer, even 'Baby'
had gone to live and work in South Africa. It had been a long-
standing wish of Beatrix's to help with the education of the Moore
children, in particular the girls, and as long ago as 1904 she had
written to Norman, 'I am going to send one of the little girls to college some day, either "Norah" of the squirrel book or "Freda" but
there is time enough yet.' Sadly, neither of them ever did go to
university and nor did 'Baby'. Beatrix's offer was put to her in such
a way that she didn't understand it. 'I was in my late teens and one
day my mother said to me, "You don't want to be a blue stocking,
do you?" I didn't know what it meant but I was frightened by the
sound of it, so I said, "No, of course not!" and I never went.'

While Beatrix had been working on her illustrations for the
Almanac she had also been doing a series of full colour animal
paintings to sell for one guinea each in order to 'raise a fund to

Noel Moore, the eldest of
Annie Moore's eight children,
and always his mother's
favourite, became an Anglo-
Catholic priest and worked in
the East End of London.

save a strip of foreshore woodland and meadow, near Windermere Ferry, from imminent risk of disfigurement by extensive building and town extension'. Many of these pictures were sold in America by those who had followed in Anne Carroll Moore's footsteps and called on Beatrix at Hill Top, and within a year enough money had been raised. 'It was a great satisfaction to me to have been able to help the fund through the kindness of my friends in America ... A dry, but unobtrusive, foot-path has been made, along the meadow and through the wood, beside the lake; it has given very great pleasure both to the residents of the town (or large village!) and to the visitors from a distance. And what especially pleases me – a large space quite out of sight behind the wood has been set apart as a parking place for cars – both private cars and these horrible motor charabancs that have done so much to spoil the Lake district ... Whenever I cross the ferry and look at the pleasant green banks I will think of the good friends across a wider stretch of water.'

Among the Americans who had contributed to the fund was a Mrs J. Templeman Coolidge of Boston who had visited Hill Top with her young son, Henry P. Coolidge, in 1927. Beatrix and Henry P. had formed a great friendship – 'That boy doesn't miss much!' – and following their meeting Beatrix started writing

By 1928 Beatrix had raised enough money (by selling animal pictures, mainly in America) to save a strip of Lake Windermere foreshore from development. This is one of her early lakeside sketches.

again. 'All my spare time last winter I was working at the guinea pig story. I became so much interested in it – it grew longer and longer, and I kept re-writing earlier chapters.' Her reawakened interest in story-telling fortuitously coincided with 'an alarming visitation, an American publisher who took the trouble to come all the way from London in search of a book that does not exist. Alexander McKay. He produces very beautifully illustrated books, there is no question about that. It would vex my old publishers very much, and I don't like breaking with old friends. Possibly I may arrange to have published something in America for the American market only.'

Frederick Warne had indeed been upset at the suggestion of Miss Potter doing a book for another publisher, but it was when Fruing Warne was ill and the company had been having certain publishing problems: 'The difficulty in our own catalogue of late years has been that the public are buying their books by weight rather than by quality, and we have had to employ of recent years, much to our distaste, a horrid, bulking antique paper on which the latest Juvenile books have been printed.' On the other hand, Mr McKay was very persuasive and by the end of 1928 Beatrix had virtually agreed to the publication of *The Fairy Caravan* in America. 'Sometimes I feel I don't want to print the stories at all, just keep them for the private edification of Henry P. and me. I guess we will keep some of them private and unprinted; they are more and more peculiar; I wonder what makes me spin such funny spider webs.'

Beatrix was worried about how she would be able to manage the illustrations. 'My eyes have lost the faculty of seeing clean colours ... I have found no assistant yet. I wrote to an art school which did not even reply, and lost time. I think you said 8 coloured; I have 3 more on hand, and another designed. Should you get 2 or 3 designed in America? *How long have I*?' But in the end she did manage to do all the drawings herself, and *The Fairy Caravan* was published by David McKay in Boston in October 1929 and was dedicated to Henry P.

Frederick Warne were angry and jealous that Beatrix had passed them over, and they wrote warning her that she might lose copyright in the book altogether if it was not published in Britain, but Beatrix felt it to be too autobiographical and revealing. 'I am shy about publishing that stuff in London.' Although she was not one to be frightened into doing something against her will, she appreciated the necessity to safeguard her copyright and, knowing that to be entirely safe she must deposit copies for registration purposes, she arranged for one hundred unbound sets of the American edition to be shipped to an Ambleside printer, where they were given an English title-page and dedication and a paper binding. After the copyright had been attended to, Beatrix gave away copies

One of Beatrix's drawings for *The Fairy Caravan*, published in America by David McKay of Philadelphia in 1929.

Troutbeck Park farmhouse as Beatrix drew it for *The Fairy Caravan*. 'The shelf is not really there, with bee hives.'

to her relatives and friends, and to her shepherds and farm workers, who at once started identifying themselves, their houses and their animals in the book, for the setting is very clearly Beatrix's beloved Lake District. Tom Storey had his precious copy readily at hand all his life, well-fingered and strengthened after much use, the pages falling open easily at the sketches of Troutbeck Park or Stoney Lane. The copies Beatrix did not give away she kept. 'Part of the 100 I intend to hoard, taking experience by the disappearance of the first editions of *Peter*.'

The book was an immediate success in America and Alexander McKay was quick to ask for a sequel. Beatrix was at first reluctant: 'You must remember that I am *not* a prolific scribbler. I wrote myself out on the rabbit series.' She also had a conscience about Frederick Warne and was anxious that any new book should be one they could publish, too; a sequel to *The Fairy Caravan* would

'Stoney Lane, Sawrey – Barn is imaginery'. *The Fairy Caravan* was not published by Frederick Warne until 1952.

hardly be appropriate. For inspiration she turned to a story that she had started nearly forty years before and had added to while she was staying in Sidmouth with her parents in 1901, a story about a pig who was sent shopping to Stymouth by his aunts Dorcas and Porcas and who ended up by going to sea.

Beatrix found it difficult working for two masters. Arthur Stephens did not like the drawings that Alexander McKay liked best and vice versa, and although *The Tale of Little Pig Robinson* was published by both Frederick Warne and David McKay in September 1930, the American edition had twelve more black-and-white drawings in it than the English one. Following publication, more than one person drew attention to the parallels in *Little Pig Robinson* to the story by Hugh Lofting of Dr Dolittle, an accusation that amused Beatrix more than somewhat as she had never heard of Dr Dolittle before she was sent a copy by an American friend. She jumped to her own defence: 'I take you solemnly to

(*above*) *The Tale of Little Pig Robinson* was published in 1930 on both sides of the Atlantic, but the American edition had twelve extra illustrations, of which this is one.

(*left*) 'Robinson and his new friend ... walked along the quay hand in hand: their appearance seemed to cause unbounded amusement.'

High Yewdale Farm, under Ivy Crag, was part of the 4,000-acre Monk Coniston Estate bought by Beatrix for the National Trust in 1930.

witness that it is my first acquaintance and meeting with Dr Dolittle and his fascinating ship's company! *I* also have taken a voyage, in imagination; and sent my Pig Robinson to the southern seas; but I think my adventures are cribbed from *Robinson Crusoe*, "per" Stevenson's *Kidnapped*. There is nothing new under the sun; and in the making of many books there are bound to be coincidences; it is probably that many plagiarisms are quite involuntary. It's a most amusing clever book (the Dr I mean to say!).'

The money that Beatrix earned from *The Fairy Caravan* and *Little Pig Robinson* came at an opportune moment, for Beatrix had been buying more land. 'After dinner Mr Heelis and I are going to Coniston. There is a lovely stretch of mountain and valley to sell there and the National Trust are trying to buy it ... I am very interested because my great grandfather had land there and I always longed to buy it back and give it to the Trust in remembrance. I was very much attached to my grandmother Jessy Crompton and said to be very like her, "only not so good looking!!" according to old folks. Perhaps I will be able to help out of this book – it would be like a fairy tale, would it not?'

Beatrix used Hill Top as a place to draw in and to relax. The spaniel is Willie's shooting dog, Spotty.

The land was the Monk Coniston Estate, an area of some 4,000 acres, which included farms and cottages, Tilberthwaite Fells and Tarn Hows, and stretched from Little Langdale to the village of Coniston. Beatrix was concerned that the estate might be split up if it was not bought by one person, and knowing that the National Trust might have difficulty in raising the money quickly, she bought it herself. Then she offered 2,000 acres of it to the Trust – at the price she had paid for it but only when they could raise the money, and she promised that eventually the rest of the estate would also come to them. The Trust accepted and quickly raised the money – then they asked Beatrix to manage the entire estate as one until such time as they could take it over. Beatrix's reputation as a farmer and sheep breeder was now considerable.

Now in her mid-sixties and managing vast areas of farmland, Beatrix was finding that the years spent out on the fells in all weathers were beginning to have an effect on her health. 'I have been in bed twice this winter already with bad colds – not serious, but just sufficiently bronchial to make me afraid of bronchitis if I live to be as old as my mother, which is unlikely.' Her mother was

ninety-one and in extremely good health. 'She is very lucky in having good lungs, no rheumatism and good eyesight.'

That year, 1930, Beatrix became the first woman president of the Herdwick Sheepbreeders Association, founded all those years before by her friend, Hardwicke Rawnsley, and she was a familiar figure at local shows, judging at some and winning prizes at others. 'Your long-suffering aunty looks rather like an elderly sheep. But I am more like a good tempered witch than a cow. We had speeches at lunch, at the Hawkshead Agricultural Show, and an old jolly farmer – replying to a "toast" – likened me – the president – to the first prize cow! He said she was a lady-like animal; and one of us had neat legs, and walked well; but I think that was the cow not me, being slightly lame. We had our pretty little Baa's at Ennerdale Show last week, and yesterday at Keswick . . . The sheep have been very successful in the female classes; 16 first prizes and several shows to come.' That same year, Beatrix won the silver challenge cup for the best Herdwick ewe in the Lake District. 'I will hold it for a year. If I take it 3 years it becomes mine; I think next year is pretty safe, as my younger sheep was never beaten – but 3 years would be a stroke of good luck! Now the autumn sheep fairs are on, we have to sell about 500, but prices are not very good. The wool is still unsold – a lot of our hardwearing Herdwick wool goes to U.S.A. for carpet making, and I am afraid trade is bad in America as well as here. It will be a hard winter, so many are out of work.'

The latest dogs in the Heelis household were Lassie, 'a Scotch colley puppy . . . too lively for anything serious at present', and

(opposite) Studies of sheep in white chalk and crayon, on brown paper. In 1930 Beatrix became the first woman president of the Herdwick Sheepbreeders' Association.

Beatrix won the silver challenge cup for the best Herdwick ewe in the Lake District in 1930. Here Geoff Storey, Tom Storey's young son, poses with a prizewinner.

Spotty, 'a fat spaniel with long ears. She is Mr Heelis's dog for going out shooting.' And amid the hurly burly of farm life and of all her other commitments Beatrix still had time to make a sad announcement of the death of a favourite ram: 'A grand old champion of the fells is dead. Mr Josiah Cockbain's celebrated Herdwick ram, "Saddleback Wedgewood", had died on Jan 14th at Hill Top Farm, Sawrey ... Wedgewood was the perfect type of hard, big boned, Herdwick tup, with strong clean legs, springy fetlocks, broad scope, fine horns, a grand jacket and mane. He had strength without coarseness. A noble animal.'

It seems amazing that Beatrix still had any time left for writing on her own behalf, but Alexander McKay had once again been pressing her for a new book and by the winter of 1931 she was telling friends in America, 'Another fit of scribbling has taken possession of me: I am trying to make a frame work to hold some more of the surplus stories that were left over from *The Fairy Caravan*,' and by the following April, 'A curious thing has happened about my next book. I wrote out so many chapters and posted them. I never had much control of my subject; it ambles along like the *Caravan* ... I remarked to Mr McKay that the book seemed likely to be over weighted by the tale of the Second Cousin Mouse; an absurd and grisly version of *Bluebeard* which grew to a big length; I suggested throwing it out. Which he has done. But he suggested printing it first as a separate book under the title of *Sister Anne*; and "eliminating the mice". Alright; it will suit me well. Only if the mice are "eliminated" the tale becomes deadly serious. I am recopying it and trying to improve the writing; but I am uncertain whether it is a romance or a joke. It certainly is not food for babes.'

An illustration by Katharine Sturges for *Sister Anne*, 'an absurd and grisly version of *Bluebeard*' by Beatrix, published only in America in 1932.

Sister Anne was published in December 1932 in America only. Beatrix had not been able to face doing the illustrations and they had been commissioned by the American publisher. They met with Beatrix's veiled approval. 'The illustrations are fine ... Do thank Katharine Sturges from me for interpreting just what I meant! She cannot draw dogs – but no more can I. I should have sent a photograph of a wolf hound; they have not *flap* ears.' The book was never published in England, though Beatrix registered copyright with an unbound American copy, and it received a cool reception from her first American friend, Anne Carroll Moore, who criticised it as unsuitable for children – a point of which Beatrix was well aware.

That Christmas was once again a trying time. 'My mother is refusing to die. She was unconscious for 4 hours yesterday, and then she suddenly asked for tea. She cannot possibly recover, and she suffers a lot of pain at times, so we hope it will soon be over; but she has wonderful vitality for any age – let alone 93.'

Greetings

From Beatrix Potter
To Anne Carroll Moore and Nicholas
with love and good wishes for a Merry Christmas
Dec. 3ᵈ 1932

Beatrix's old friend, Anne Carroll Moore (with her doll Nicholas), was remembered in this card from Beatrix that Christmas, even though she had criticized *Sister Anne* severely.

Mrs Potter's cook, Lucissa, feels that Beatrix was less sympathetic than perhaps she might have been. 'When Mrs Potter was dying she was more concerned about her Herdwicks and the farm she had. She said, "I just can't waste my time here." She even started to take things out of the sitting-room before she had died. There was no love lost between mother and daughter ... Mrs Potter was never what you might call ill. She just died of old age, she just gradually passed away.'

Helen Potter died on 20 December 1932 and was buried near her family home in Lancashire. Beatrix was faced with clearing up the

Benjamin Dawson, the Lindeth How gardener. After old Mrs Potter died in December 1932, Beatrix wrote references for all her mother's employees.

house and with answering the letters that poured in. 'She was wonderfully clear in mind, but ... I am glad she is at rest.' Mrs Potter left Lucissa £50 in her will, a considerable sum in those days, and the servants were 'given a month's notice or you could leave if you could get another post. Mrs Heelis would give you a reference.' Beatrix's reference for the gardener was fulsome and typical of those she gave: 'I have much pleasure in recommending Benjamin Dawson. He was nine years in the service of my mother ... He has been accustomed to herbacious border, some bedding out, green house, peach house, early vegetables, and the use of the motor lawn mower ... Mrs Potter had a high opinion of Ben's usefulness. He is a thoroughly reliable man, and strong in health.' As Beatrix

commented in a letter at the time, her mother's death marked the end of an era. 'My mother's long life was a link with times that are passed away, though still vivid in our memory – the old leisurely pleasant days of stately carriage horses, and of the Keswick coach.'

Beatrix returned with some relief to farming, exchanging details of cattle prices, hay yields and the excesses of farm workers' wages with her two great farming friends, her cousin Caroline and her sister-in-law Mary. Mary had continued to run the farm after Bertram's death until 1935 when she let it, together with the farm-house, and lived on in the house at Ashyburn with her niece, Hetty. Beatrix was very fond of Mary – 'She was a nice Scotch body; homely quiet and sensible' – and she and Willie went to stay with her in Ashyburn every August Bank Holiday weekend until Mary's death in 1939.

After a hard day's work, Beatrix and Willie liked nothing better than to walk on the fells above Sawrey together, often going up the bridlepath from Castle Cottage, past meadows full of buttercups, marshes with forget-me-nots and marsh cups, and with foxgloves and tormentil flowering beside the path, until they reached Moss Eccles Tarn perched above the village. Beatrix had bought the tarn

Moss Eccles Tarn, above the village of Sawrey, is still the peaceful haven today that it was for Beatrix and Willie Heelis.

at the time she bought Castle Cottage, and they had planted water lilies in it and stocked it with fish. There was a boat in the old boathouse and they sat together for hours, Willie fishing and Beatrix watching the fish leaping from the calm water or the mallards splashing by the rhododendron-covered banks, a fox barking harshly from the nearby woods. It was a magic place, far from the hurly-burly of books and publishing, or the troubles and stresses of family life.

Beatrix no longer listened to the pleas from London and Boston for a new book. 'I am "written out" for storybooks, and my eyes are tired for painting, but I can still take great and useful pleasure in old oak – and drains – and old roofs – and damp walls – oh the repairs! ... Such are the problems that occupy my declining years! I am 68; we both had colds; it rains and rains and rains and is nearly dark. Things might be worse.'

The 'little books' were continuing their successful path, selling in their thousands, not only in the English language but in translation, too. By 1934 *The Tale of Peter Rabbit* was available in

The water lilies planted by Beatrix still flower and multiply today among the fish in Moss Eccles Tarn.

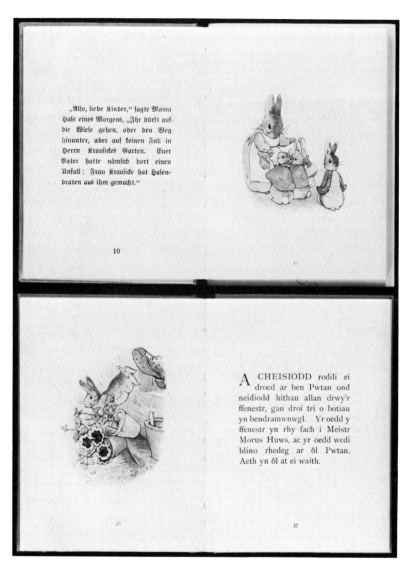

By 1934 *Peter Rabbit* had been translated into six languages, including German (in both English and Gothic types) and Welsh.

French (*Pierre Lapin*), Dutch (*Het Verhaal van Pieter Langoor*), Welsh (*Hanes Pwtan y Gwningen*), German in both English and Gothic types (*Die Geschichte des Peterchen Hase*), Spanish (*Pedrin El Conejo Travieso*) and Afrikaans (*Die Verhaal van Pieter Konyntjie*). The name of Beatrix Potter had become known all over the world.

It was at this time that Graham Greene published an essay devoted entirely to her. 'The obvious characteristic of Beatrix Potter's style is selective realism, which takes emotion for granted and puts aside love and death with a gentle detachment reminiscent of Mr E. M. Forster's'; and he expounded the theory that 'At some time between 1907 and 1909 Miss Potter must have passed through an emotional ordeal which changed the character of her genius. It would be impertinent to inquire into the nature of the ordeal. Her case is curiously similar to that of Henry James. Something happened which shook their faith in appearance,' and it accounted for the 'dark period of Miss Potter's art' expressed in Mr Drake Puddle-duck, Mr Jackson, Samuel Whiskers and Mr Tod. Beatrix seldom entered into correspondence with her critics, but in Mr Greene's case she could not hold back and wrote to tell him that she had in fact been suffering from flu when writing Mr Tod, rather than from any emotional disturbance, and that she deprecated sharply 'the Freudian school' of criticism.

Beatrix kept up a regular correspondence with her American friends and they continued to visit her, though less frequently now that everyone was getting older, and they sent her a continuous flow of books to read. She was finding that with frequent colds and chills and with the onset of lumbago and rheumatism she had more time for reading than since her early childhood. She was particularly enjoying her discovery of 'new' American writers. 'Please send another of Willa Cather's. I just have Shadows on the Rock ... I think I never read a more beautifully written book. The atmosphere, and character drawing are perfect.' There were also children's books on which her librarian friends wanted her opinion, and Beatrix was much interested and most appreciative. 'The writers take more pains with juvenile literature in America ... In the main children's literature has not been taken seriously over here, too much left to the appeal of gaudy covers and binding, and the choice of toy sellers.'

Beatrix also kept in close touch with the various strands of Willie's large family, visiting the sick and elderly, keenly observing the young, and now and then interfering but with the best of intentions. When Willie's nephew died suddenly in 1933 at the early age of forty-four leaving a young family, Beatrix was concerned for his young son. 'I was at prep school,' John Heelis recalls, 'and a week after my father died Aunt Beatrix arrived at school in an upright motor car, driven by an ancient chauffeur. "I've come to see the headmaster," she announced. "I'm taking John Heelis away from the school. I know they can't afford to keep him here." The headmaster was a quick thinker. He sent me out for a walk with matron and then telephoned my mother to discover that she had already paid for the full term and didn't want me to leave at all! It was misguided kindness on Aunt Beatrix's part and typical of her that she never thought she might be upsetting anybody. What I now know is that she wanted to put me into a school at Windermere which she would pay for – about which no doubt she had already made a special arrangement concerning fees with the headmaster.'

Beatrix's cousin, Stephanie, and her husband Kenneth Duke came with their family to stay in Sawrey every summer holidays. For their two small girls, Rosemary and Jean, it was a visit they looked forward to with great excitement. 'I caught my first fish in Moss Eccles Tarn,' Jean Duke (now Jean Holland) remembers. 'We loved going there. Willie and Cousin B were very kind to us. I used to collect cigarette cards and Willie allowed me to open all his precious tobacco tins, which he bought in bulk, in order to get the cards out. We used to go out in one or other of the old cars – they had two then – with the old chauffeur, Walter, driving in front of a glass panel and us in the back where they often used to put a sheep or two. There were holes in the roof of one car where it had perished and if it was raining we used to put up an umbrella inside!

'The back of Castle Cottage was stacked with stuff that Cousin B had kept from Aunt Helen's house, pictures and so on, and with bales of tweed woven from her Herdwick sheep. When we were there one year a rather earnest couple came to play over one of Cousin B's books they had set to music. There was a grand piano in the end room and, after the main part was over, the visitors played their setting of the Twenty-third Psalm. When they had

(above left) Beatrix concerned herself with the affairs of the Heelis family. This is John Heelis and his young brother, David, in 1933.

(above right) In that same summer of 1933 Willie photographed Jean Duke, the daughter of Beatrix's cousin, with her first fish, caught in Moss Eccles Tarn.

Stephanie Duke, the cousin to whom Beatrix had dedicated *Jeremy Fisher* in 1906. Many years later Stephanie awakened Beatrix's interest in Pekinese dogs.

finished, Cousin B turned to my father and said, "Waters of comfort makes me think of brandy. Would you like some, Kenneth?"

'We were also there in 1936 when a letter arrived from Walt Disney asking for permission to make a film of *Peter Rabbit*. Cousin B was not at all keen on the idea. "My drawings are not good enough," she remarked. "To make Silly Symphonies they will have to enlarge them and that will show up all the imperfections."

'My mother had a Pekinese dog which she took everywhere with her and of which Cousin B was always very scathing, "Stupid little dogs, Pekes." However, one day our dog climbed Helvellyn with us and Cousin B was so impressed with her energy and courage that she decided to get a Peke herself and asked my mother for a puppy.'

Beatrix was delighted with her new acquisition which she called Tzusee. 'We have a queer little animal here, a small female Pekinese, a very "heathen Chinese" for mischief and naughtiness, but engaging and affectionate. The colleys don't like her; she is impertinent.' Within a few months she had a second puppy, Chuleh: 'I have always despised foreign dogs; but these are both spirited and affectionate, and less trouble than terriers, as they get sufficient play and exercise in the garden.' Beatrix and Willie became very attached to the Pekes and hated being separated from them. The dogs were given complete freedom of the house and even slept on the bed at night.

For many years Beatrix had been writing regularly to Ivy Hunt, the little girl who had delivered her mother's hats to Bolton Gardens, and who was now living in the United States with her husband, Jack Steel, and their twelve-year-old daughter, June. Shortly after her seventieth birthday, Beatrix arranged and paid for Ivy and June to visit their relations in Scotland and to come on to Sawrey, crossing the Atlantic in one of the smaller ships. 'These very grand ships with swimming pools and extremely quick passages are the last word of luxury; but surely an 8 days passage in a not-the-very-fashionablest would be alright, provided it were tourist class.' Their visit was a great success and it gave Beatrix much pleasure to reminisce with Ivy about those far-off days in London.

Beatrix was entering her seventies in good heart. 'I do not resent older age; if it brings slowness it brings experience and weight ... I have felt curiously better and younger this last 12 months! Last year I felt peaky it was irksome. I mind it little (with one or two reservations). For one thing to quote a friend, "Thank God I have

(*above left*) Beatrix had two Pekes, Tzusee and Chuleh, which she and Willie loved dearly and hated being separated from.

(*above right*) When Beatrix and Willie went away they left their dogs next door with another Peke called Yummi.

Yew Tree Farm was one of the
Monk Coniston Estate farms
Beatrix returned to the
National Trust for management
when she reached seventy.

the seeing eye", that is to say, as I lie in bed I can walk step by step
on the fells and rough lands seeing every stone and flower and
patch of bog and cotton pass where my old legs will never take me
again. Also do you not feel it is rather pleasing to be so much *wiser*
than quantities of young idiots? ... I begin to assert myself at 70.
What worries me at times is so many dependents ... It is a pity that
the wisdom and experience of old age is largely wasted – (except in
the case of judges who sit for ever, usually without falling into
dotage).'

Beatrix did feel, however, that the time had come to divest herself of some of her responsibilities, and as the National Trust had
just appointed a new agent, Bruce Thompson, she handed back to
him the management of the Trust's Monk Coniston farms. The
transfer was not easy; Bruce Thompson was new to the job and
for the past six years Beatrix had been running things in her own
particular way. The farm tenants found it hard to accept anyone
else as their landlord, and they continued to approach her, rather
than the Trust, with their problems. For the next few years Beatrix
was involved in an almost weekly, not always harmonious, correspondence with Bruce Thompson about repairing roofs, installing
new drains and planting trees.

chapter six

'It is some years ago since I have walked
on the beloved hills but I remember every
stone and rock – and stick.'

Beatrix at her home in Sawrey, aged seventy-seven

By THE FOLLOWING year, 1938, the storm clouds of war were gathering once again over Europe. Hitler's move into parts of Czechoslovakia in the summer worried Beatrix as much as it worried everyone else, and she did not care for the man. 'Now one has a feeling of stupefaction. Anything – "nearly" anything – may be better than war. It is not an honourable fear – and doubtful whether it has any permanency. Can you hear Hitler over the wireless as far as America? Did you ever hear such a brutal, raving lunatic. I could not understand a word of his clipped rapid German; but the ranting note and the smiling face in the tele-graphed photographs are not sane.'

She did not think much of Mr Chamberlain either. 'If Mr Chamberlain believes his promises he must be an incurable opti-mist ... We do not like Mr Chamberlain. He could do no other than give in at Munich – things were in such a helpless muddle; whose fault?? and there is not a clear case for the Sudetan question or for the Czechs. The serious thing is his want of any proper sense of responsibility *now*.'

Though far from the centre of international strife, Beatrix and Willie were, like everyone else in Britain, involved in preparations for war, 'We did not take gas masks very seriously in this remote district; which was just as well for our peace of mind as they were supplied wrong size – so few small and medium compared with the large size that the police sensibly decided it would be best to with-draw them.'

'We did not take gas masks very seriously in this remote district,' wrote Beatrix to an American friend during the Munich crisis of 1938.

A branch of apple blossom in water-colour and pen-and-ink. As well as all her other responsibilities Beatrix had been clearing the orchard of an old house she had bought. In March 1939 her health broke down.

Before the year was out Beatrix was in hospital. She had been having a good deal of pain and a certain amount of bleeding and, after seeing her doctor in Liverpool, went straight into hospital for a minor operation. She was away from Sawrey for only ten days, however, and on her return she was soon as busy as ever.

The following February Beatrix and Willie journeyed to Scotland for Mary Potter's funeral, leaving the Pekes with Miss Hammond and Miss Mills, who themselves had taken yet another of the Peke litter, Yummi. 'I hope the little dogs are well behaved and not too disconsolate. Chuleh was dribbling tears during the packing; Tzuzee aloof, grave in disapproval. Our clothes are sniffed by terriers at hotels.'

Shortly after they came back from Scotland Beatrix was faced with the Herculean task of clearing out the badly neglected house and garden of a colourful and eccentric American friend, Rebecca Owen, who had lived near Hawkshead for many years and who died early in 1939 in Rome. On her last visit from Italy Miss Owen had sold her fine old Georgian house, Belmont Hall, to Beatrix and Willie. 'The house is scarcely habitable, though it seems a pity to let it fall in – fall *down* it will not. Georgian building stone. Perhaps some time it might be repaired for a hostel ... I have a free hand in an old *walled* garden of over an acre. The old fan-trained fruit trees in the last stage of old age. I have planted some clematis against them, and some shrubs, such as ceanothus, between, to gradually grow into their place. Is chimonanthus fragrans a bush that would grow? I have witch hazel, and shrubby spiraeas, and syringas.'

Before her operation, Beatrix wrote to her friends of her gratitude at having 'seen the snowdrops again'. This is one of her early water-colours.

Working in the old house and garden, managing the farms, chairman of the Nursing Trust, running about from morning to night, Beatrix was doing too much, and within three months from her first visit there she was back in the Women's Hospital in Liverpool. 'I am not particularly pleased to be having a complete anaesthetic; otherwise I am entirely indifferent, he said I would be out in 3 days. He says the place is difficult to get at – right in the opening to the bladder, and that it would be too difficult and painful without complete anaesthetic ... There are 2 other women in the small ward; one very cheerful party who seems to have had vast experience; and another – the wife of a sea-captain-mate or engineer, who is a bundle of nerves. She admits to smoking 300 cigarettes per week ... The nurses and sister seem very pleasant. There is great want of an open window, and very hot with hot pipes.'

Beatrix was not out in three days, however, as promised, and it was decided that another operation was necessary and urgent, this time to remove her womb altogether. The night before the operation she wrote to her dear friends next door. 'What a mess! but not intirely without premonition. I have failed in strength more than people know this last 2 years. Most times it has been an effort to walk to Hill Top. I am so glad I was feeling particularly well last week; and I have seen the snowdrops again. If it was not for poor W I would be indifferent to the result. It is such a wonderfully easy going under; and in some ways preferable to a long invalidism, with only old age to follow. Moreover the whole world seems to be rushing to Armageddon. But not even Hitler can damage the fells.'

Beatrix had also made plans about the future. 'If I do not return Wm will have a list of things that I want eventually to go to Hill Top after his death ... I hope that Cecily and Wm will walk out little dogs on Sundays; they are old enough to face comment! *Could* she learn picquet or could you play 3 handed whist? It would be far best for the poor man to follow Willy Gaddum's example and remarry, provided he did not make a fool of himself by marrying, or not marrying, a servant. The misfortune is that I have acquiesced in such slovenly untidyness and unpunctuality that I am afraid no old maidly lady would put up with it and he is too old to remodel. So I hope and feel sure you will do your best for him in the winter evenings. I have very great confidence in the good sense and kindness of both of you ... Much love to you both and to Yummi.'

The list Beatrix left with Willie was in addition to her will which she had also made, and it was just as precise, with clear instructions as to where everything was to go. Most of her books and watercolours to be given to libraries and galleries: 'I should prefer any watercolours to be given to a public collection rather than

Beatrix asked Miss Hammond and Miss Mills to look after Willie and the Pekes should she not return from hospital.

sold; likewise the Caldecott pen and inks.' The furniture was to be retained in particular houses: 'I would like certain favourite pieces of furniture to be kept for Hill Top (in the event of it seeming likely that my rooms there are preserved).' And Beatrix did not forget her animals. 'No old horse or worn out dog to be sold; either given to a really trustworthy person or put down.'

Willie wrote to the National Trust, to inform them of his wife's anticipated operation and with her instructions about certain properties, adding the warning that 'she wants the whole matter kept absolutely quiet'. As always, Beatrix did not want any fuss.

Willie was in Liverpool with her and for some days following the operation Beatrix was gravely ill, but within two weeks she was sitting up in bed and writing letters again. 'I have survived, and feel supremely silly. The surgeon says I shall be cured, which remains to be seen. At all events, it can never happen again, "a pretty complete removal at an unusually advanced age." ... To think that I had wound up and arranged everything – even to inquiring whether there is a crematorium in Liverpool (which is inconvenient in the Lake district) and now it is all at large again.' Then in typical down-to-earth conclusion: 'As to whether I am thankful I refuse to make any observation before seeing how it lasts –'

By June, approaching her seventy-third birthday, Beatrix was almost back to her old form. 'I am incredibly well considering the short time since the operation. The only thing I complain of now is swelling in my ankles, which I hope is only temporary weakness through not using them for so long.' She began to get about again. 'I went to the Troutbeck sheep farm this morning and watched the

The operation successfully over, Beatrix returned to Sawrey and within three months was back watching the men clipping her beloved Herdwicks. This recent photograph was taken in Little Langdale.

men clipping, and afterwards herd the cattle, driven into the "West fold", a fine sight, about 30 black cows with their calves at foot, and a magnificent white bull. He is a lovely beast and so far he is very quiet.'

The country was preparing itself for war. 'Neighbours busy stitching black stuff for blinds. I have my dark curtains, rather moth eaten, from last war. I suppose it's the same all over. The black-outs have been held late, after people have put their lights out; to save inconvenience. It's difficult to strike a mean. It seems like playing at being ready for war; and neither the Germans nor *us* know whether we are serious.' And Beatrix was not the only person in the country who was uncertain what plans to make: 'Whether to lay in much stores or not? I have got a lot of sugar ... and I have got a store of biscuits for my 2 little dogs.'

War was declared on 3 September 1939, and it could not have been more inconveniently timed for the farming community. 'This is always a busy time, the sheep fairs are in Sept. and October. Shows are starting, but of course came to an end when war began.' Beatrix and Willie bought a pony cart to help their petrol ration go further, and they suddenly found that much of their time was spent in conforming to the new war-time regulations. 'The continual filling up of forms and gradings and papers is a nuisance; everything that farmers produce has to be arranged for marketing so that the Govt. knows what there will be to draw upon for supplies.' Beatrix was irritated by the whole business, as she was increasingly irritated by the National Trust in the form of Bruce Thompson, with whom she took issue on a matter relating to woodlands in the Lake District. This, however, was a quarrel that could not be allowed to develop, for the Trust knew well that Beatrix intended to give them much of her property on her death, and the 'top brass' were summoned from London. That particular irritation was eased.

Shortly after the outbreak of war, Beatrix received a *cri de coeur* from the wife of her second cousin, Sir William Hyde Parker, in whose beautiful family house in Suffolk, Melford Hall, she had first stayed over forty years before. Sir William had been badly injured in an accident in the black-out, his Danish wife Ulla had recently given birth to their daughter, Beth, and Melford Hall had been commandeered by the army. The family were homeless. Could Beatrix possibly help? Beatrix, as usual, rose to the occasion and arranged for them to stay at a hotel in Sawrey, but it was soon apparent that they needed somewhere quieter and more private. Beatrix handed them the keys of Hill Top.

It had been a difficult decision for her to take, for she had allowed no one to live there since she and Willie had moved to Castle Cottage, and Hill Top was full of her most precious possessions. Now she was allowing a family of three adults and two

Beatrix invited her cousin, Sir William Hyde Parker, who was recuperating from an accident, to bring his family to Hill Top – and she photographed them by the porch.

Hill Top was 'Tom Kitten's house' and the Hyde Parkers spent many happy months there – in considerable contrast to their life at Melford Hall.

children (the Hyde Parkers had brought Nanny to look after two-year-old Richard and the baby) into the place that she had kept so exclusively to herself over the years, the place she thought of as her museum. It was, on the other hand, a solution to something that had been giving her a good deal of worry, the very real possibility that Hill Top could be commandeered at any time by the authorities to house a family evacuated from a nearby town. She put away her most precious and fragile treasures and 'sent over the big spare bed and sundry furniture and etc.', and the Hyde Parkers settled in to a rather more primitive life than they had been used to in Melford Hall but one for which they were extremely grateful. Sir William spent much of his time fishing with Willie on Moss Eccles Tarn, and the rest of the family often called to see Beatrix at Castle Cottage or invited her to tea at Hill Top. Beatrix enjoyed having them there. 'The Parkers are in Tom Kitten's "house". They are dear little children . . . Richard aged 3 is a pickle.'

The first few months of the war made little impact on Sawrey. 'We see a good deal of activity overhead being near the coast, but so far no raids have come so far as the west coast, and every one runs out when we hear a plane.' During the winter both Beatrix and Willie were victims of the influenza epidemic that was sweeping the country, but the bitterly cold winter was followed by a glorious spring. 'The bluebells are very lovely and the hawthorn blossom like snow on the green hedges and the cuckoo calling; a world of beauty that will survive – and Freedom will survive, whatever happens to us.'

By June Britain was reeling from the retreat from Dunkirk. 'We are living through an anxious time. Last week was horrible. Then there was a reaction of relief and pride when the B.E.F. got out of Flanders. Now there is another reaction of anxiety when we reflect upon the loss of guns and transport vehicles.' Beatrix was angry that America had not offered help, though she realised that her librarian friends were not directly to blame. 'I have hardly patience to write a letter to the U.S.A. I know the New Englanders would have helped old England if their hands had not been tied politically . . . Surely U.S.A. might have sent us aeroplanes and guns without becoming publicly involved in European war . . . American help is not going to be in time to turn the scale before August.'

Like everyone Beatrix was becoming concerned about the dangers of an invasion by Hitler and like so many she was investigating the possibilities of sending some children out of the country. 'I am not intending to bolt! What ever happens! I am thinking of two school girls, a cousin's daughters.' Beatrix suggested to Stephanie and Kenneth Duke that Rosemary and Jean might go to America, where she had so many friends who would look after them and where her books were earning considerable royalties

Unlike these properly dressed wardens, Willie, a reserve policeman, was issued with a tin hat which he refused to wear.

that could be used to support them. She made elaborate plans for them and for two other children to go to friends in Philadelphia, but there were difficulties over permits and before they could get passages the immediate danger seemed past. 'There is a great change of feeling – a complete recovery of confidence compared to that black ten days. And the delay has been invaluable. I may not tell you how martial we feel even here!'

Beatrix and Willie were doing what they could for the war effort. Willie was on the War Agricultural Committee and a reserve policeman. 'He has a "tin hat", which he refuses to wear – until Hitler comes! ... I doubt his standing the weather later on. He is only on near-by roads, looking for windows not properly black[ed] out, and motor offenders, to help the regular police, and to learn their duties in case they have to go elsewhere.'

Beatrix, leaning on her stick, was a familiar figure at local shows. Here she is judging Herdwicks at Keswick.

Beatrix had reluctantly to admit that she was getting old. 'I cannot work like last war time, when I fed the calves and pigs and poultry; but I can get about and look after things, which is more than I expected . . . I am rather infirm on my legs, and more bowed than ever.' Although she now walked with a stick, she still managed to visit her farms regularly, to supervise the harvesting and to ensure that her sheep and cattle maintained their high standards. Together with Miss Mills she started breeding rabbits, partly to ensure that the dogs would not be short of food but also to help out with their own meat ration. Occasionally the far-off sounds of war could be heard in Sawrey, but more often than not it was the grumbling of a returning enemy bomber that interrupted the silence of the fells. 'If it were not so painful to think and know of the suffering which is taking place, a distant raid is rather fine – droning of planes very high overhead, gunfire and shells like falling stars – not at all near here – a cock pheasant shouting in the woods; our air warden, a fussy old man, blowing a whistle and ringing a hand bell; the special constable vainly requesting females to go indoors, which nobody did on a fine moonlight night. We are still waiting to see a dogfight.'

For some time now Beatrix had had little contact with Frederick Warne other than regular royalty payments on the continuing and very healthy sale of her books, but in 1941 she received a letter from Arthur Stephens saying that Warne were considering a cheap

edition of the little books. Beatrix warmly welcomed the idea and even suggested that they might consider going back to the black-and-white version of *Peter Rabbit*, provided that the colour edition was kept in print as well. In the end, however, it was decided to keep only the colour edition in print, remaking all the colour blocks and sending a duplicate set to Warne in New York so that they could print their own editions of the books there. There was still enough paper available but it was difficult to get books bound with binders losing their men to the Armed Forces.

Air raids, too, were taking their toll of men and of books. After one whole edition of *Peter Rabbit* was lost when the printers suffered a direct hit, Beatrix agreed that the original drawings for all the books should be sent to Sawrey for safe keeping. 'No place is safe, but the chances of any individual house being hit is small in the country. An isolated farmhouse has been destroyed, with 11 killed, in consequence of army lorries with lights on a main road. The lorries were not hit. There were bombers over head all night long, we are on a "route" here, they fly over and come back; and to judge by the noise some go lost and wander round ... I hope Bedford Street is still standing.' It was, though the staff frequently had to stop work and go down to the basement air-raid shelter when the roof-spotters sounded a warning bell.

Beatrix knew that the books were in demand and selling well but she was amazed in May 1942 to receive an enormous royalty

Hill Top Farm, like many other farms in the country in the 1940s, helped to ease wartime shortages by setting up silos to hold fodder for their stock.

cheque. 'Prodigious! When one thinks of the paper and the string and the wrapping up that must have been expended on the distribution of nearly two hundred thousand copies – what about war work? The world goes mad on astronomical figures. You must have had a worritting year. Such a result could not be achieved at any time without so much work; this last year it is a triumph.'

The news of Pearl Harbor and of America joining the war meant that Beatrix's letters to her American friends need no longer be critical or regretful. She had kept in regular contact, sending them letters full of news of war-time Britain, of her interpretation of the progress of the war in Europe, and of the more domestic happenings on the farms and in the village. They in turn had continued to send her books and they were now sending food parcels. 'Your charming present arrived unexpectedly this morning – *Lemon Juice*! Also butter, dextrose, onion flakes, chocolate, bacon and cheese. I was very thankful for a tin of lemon juice in a Christmas parcel . . . It helped my cough when I had bronchitis all through the month of May (which is too good a month to waste when one is nearly 76). I am not coughing now, so I shall save your lemon juice till next winter, and sprinkle the dextrose on my breakfast porridge, to promote energy as promised on the label.'

The editor of the American publication, *The Horn Book Magazine*, first approached Beatrix in 1925 for information about herself and her books, an interest that has continued ever since.

It was from America that Beatrix received most of her fan mail. 'I have been surprised at the number – and the friendliness – of the packets of dozens of letters from [the] U.S.A., and they are only a few tied up in bundles from amongst the numbers received through many years. I don't receive English letters like that – a good many from children, some wanting autographs, some enthusiastic, grateful parents (also in U.S.A.). But never does anyone outside your perfidiously complimentary nation write to tell me that I write good prose!'

Towards the end of 1940 Beatrix had received a letter from the editor of the American publication concerned with 'books and reading for children and young people', *The Horn Book Magazine*, Mrs Bertha Mahoney Miller, whom she had never met but with whom she had been corresponding regularly since 1926. Mrs Miller was asking if she would look again at a piece she wrote in 1929 for *The Horn Book* about the origins of *Peter Rabbit*, and it started Beatrix musing about the whole phenomenon. 'I have never quite understood the secret of Peter's perennial charm. Perhaps it is because he and his little friends keep on their way, busily absorbed with their own doings. They were always independent. Like Topsy – they just "grow'd". Their names especially seemed to be inevitable! I never knew a gardener named "McGregor". Several bearded horticulturalists have resented the nickname, but I do not know how it came about, nor why "Peter" was called "Peter". It is regrettable that a small boy once inquired audibly

OF BOOKS AND READING
FOR CHILDREN AND
YOUNG PEOPLE

T H E
Horn Book
MAGAZINE

October, 1955

Celebrating "The Art of Beatrix Potter"

Along the Road to Kansas by Doris Gates

Subscription price, $4.00. Single copies, $1.00.

whether the Apostle was Peter Rabbit? There is great difficulty in finding, or inventing, names void of all possible embarrassment. A few of the characters were harmless skits or caricatures, but "Mr McGregor" was not one of them, and the backgrounds of *Peter Rabbit* are of mixed locality.

'"Squirrel Nutkin" lived on the shore of Derwentwater Lake near Keswick, and "Mrs Tiggy-winkle" in the nearby village of Newlands. "Jemima Puddle-duck", "Jeremy Fisher", and others lived at Sawrey in the southern part of the English lake district.'

Beatrix once again dug out her old portfolio and in it discovered stories that she had started and never finished and pieces that she had pruned from *The Fairy Caravan*. One of these unfinished stories, *Wag-by-Wall*, a strange tale about an old woman and a black kettle, she also sent to Mrs Miller who asked if Beatrix would finish it for publication in *The Horn Book*. Beatrix was delighted and spent what time she could spare during the next year rewriting and polishing it.

In spite of the war, there were still visitors to the Lake District in holiday times and one day, early in the war, Beatrix had been visited by a man asking permission to photograph Hill Top. Reginald Hart was an architect, working at that time in the Ministry of Works in Blackpool, granting permits for building and the allocation of materials. He was also interested in china and a collector of children's books, in particular of Randolph Caldecott, and he had brought his wife and small daughter, Alison, to Sawrey to see the real houses and gardens that appeared in the pictures in Beatrix Potter's books, and which he had traced, book by book, on a visit earlier that year. Beatrix had welcomed the family into her house, signed all Alison's books, and taken Reginald Hart to see her china collection and the Caldecott originals for *The Mad Dog* which she had inherited from her father and which hung on the walls upstairs.

The Harts returned to Sawrey twice after the first visit. They always called at Castle Cottage, and they were always given a warm welcome. Reginald Hart was able to help Beatrix get her applications for building plans past the worst of the red tape and to the right quarters without delay, and he was ready to help in other directions. 'He is an immensely tall, thin man with lengthy limbs like a gibbon monkey. He hung up some plates – old blue delph – opposite my bed last time he and his family were on holiday. It was comical to see him reach up to the picture rail without the stepladder. Mrs Hart is short and shy; Alison is a little dear.'

Five-year-old Alison was less interested in the creator of the Peter Rabbit books than in her dogs, Chuleh and Tzusee, and Beatrix handed her a piece of chocolate to give to them. Alison's mother still remembers her amazement that it apparently never

In an article for *The Horn Book* in 1929 Beatrix made it clear that she 'never knew a gardener named "McGregor"'!

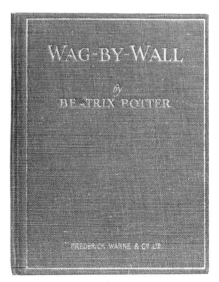

Wag-by-Wall, originally part of *The Fairy Caravan*, was published first in *The Horn Book* in 1940, then in book form in the U.S.A. only in 1944.

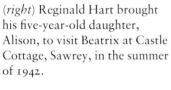

(*right*) Reginald Hart brought his five-year-old daughter, Alison, to visit Beatrix at Castle Cottage, Sawrey, in the summer of 1942.

(*below*) Her chairmanship of the Herdwick Sheepbreeders' Association had taken Beatrix into unexpected places over the years, 'usually in a tavern(!) after a sheep fair'. This was the Hawkshead Show Committee of 1922.

In spite of wartime restrictions, Beatrix continued her involvement with Herdwick sheep and was often a judge at local meetings and shows.

occurred to Beatrix to offer any chocolate to the child, a war-baby for whom sweets were a rare enough treat.

Reginald Hart had photographed Alison and Beatrix with the dogs the previous year and one of the photographs pleased Beatrix so much that she asked for more copies to send to America. 'The square shaped picture where she is looking down, just commencing to smile, and I am holding Chuleh's paw is lovely . . . It's very good of my lace edged cap (which seems to have hitched forward over my nose) and not too bad of the old woman!'

Beatrix only regretted that the photograph was not of Tzusee, 'but she is very proud and objects to being photographed'. Poor Chuleh had recently lost an eye while chasing rabbits on a walk with Willie, 'We were more upset than Chuleh. It does not show a great deal, and she is rabbiting again. Tzusee was very shocked and rather unkind – if her poor sister went near her, she got up and turned away. I don't know if she will ever wash its face again; it would be useful now.'

The winter of 1942–3 was wet rather than cold, conditions that particularly suited Herdwick sheep with their 'hard water-proof jackets', and Beatrix was pleased with the way things were going. Sheep prices were fixed at a price two to three times higher than normal by the government who bought all her wool, 'reported to be for khaki and a rumour that the cloth is going to Russia. I wish very much it may be true; and lasting!' In addition, there was a subsidy to help hill sheep, 'so hill sheep farms are paying reasonably well'. Beatrix and Willie had survived the winter and spring with only the usual colds and flu, and in addition to their own work, they were both much involved in committees. 'I am in the chair at Herdwick Breeders' Association meetings. You would

The Girl Guides camped in Sawrey throughout the war, and Beatrix happily posed for snapshots with those on cooking duty.

laugh to see me, amongst the other old farmers – usually in a tavern(!) after a sheep fair.' The very hot, early summer brought a record hay crop; it also heralded the return of the Girl Guides.

Beatrix was always glad to see them and had continued to allow them the use of her land for camping through the war. Miss Brownlow, the County Camp Adviser, knew Beatrix well and recalls those days with much affection. 'Mrs Heelis allowed the Guides to camp under some trees she had planted, so the tents could be camouflaged from the air, and she handed one of the girls an axe telling her to cut down any trees that were in the way! Every week of the school holidays we had fifty children in camp, many of them from depressed city areas, some not getting enough to eat on the rather strict rationing. When Mrs Heelis saw them arrive, she turned to me and said quietly, "A sheep shall die tonight." She liked young people very much but they had to be disciplined and well-behaved children. She had no time at all for some of the unruly children in the district who used to pinch her apples.

'Once she took a party of Guides to Hill Top to show them her treasures. In the front bedroom there was an old spinet and when she heard that one of the girls played the organ she suggested that we had a sing-song "as we used to in the old days". She sat on the large iron bedstead and we sang every camp song we could think of; then we went on to nursery rhymes and to hymns, and still she wanted more. The only way we could stop her was by breaking into "God Save the King"! She enjoyed it so much.'

The Guides who were in camp on 27 July 1943 learned quite by chance that the following day was Beatrix's seventy-seventh birthday, and they decided that they would go and greet her at Castle Cottage dressed as characters from her books, wearing whatever was available in camp. There were Jemima Puddle-ducks with feet made from cereal packets, the camp's complete supply having been emptied out and left to soften in a large bowl; there were Pigling Blands sporting pink blankets with gas-mask snouts; and the Mrs Tiggy-winkles had sewn larch needles on to grey blankets to make prickles. Beatrix was both pleased and flattered as each child stepped forward to wish her a happy birthday, and when they had gone she had to write to Warne for a new consignment of books. 'Some of them were lovely – I had to give prizes lavishly.'

In November Bertha Mahoney Miller wrote to ask if Beatrix would mind if the publication of *Wag-by-Wall* was held back until the following year so that it could be included in *The Horn Book*'s twentieth anniversary issue in May. 'I cordially agree with the delay until May . . . It leaves time to see proofs, and I would like to make it as nearly word-perfect as I know how, for the credit of your 20th anniversary.'

Beatrix was to see neither proofs nor the reprinted story. She had been ill since September with bronchitis and her heart was troubling her. 'As my heart has never been normal since I had rheumatic fever as a girl – I don't think much about it, and I was often worse in London. But if an old person of 77 continues to play these games – well it can be done once too often. I have plenty to do indoors and the little dogs are great company – most efficient foot warmers.' The weather had turned cold and snow had already reached even the bottom of the fells by the middle of November. 'It is some years ago since I have walked on the beloved hills, but I remember every stone and rock – and *stick*. I think it is pleasanter to remember an old stunted thorn or holly than to go to the spot and find it gone. The hills will last a very long time – though not for ever.'

When Beatrix was confined to bed with bronchitis in the winter of 1943, she saw her beloved Lake District country-side clearly in her mind's eye.

On the morning of 22 December 1943 Beatrix's shepherd, Tom Storey, was met by the housekeeper, Mrs Rogerson. 'She asked me to come down that evening as Mrs Heelis wanted to see me,' Tom remembered. 'The old lady was in a large bed in the end room of Castle Cottage and though I knew she was ill I was very shocked by the sight of her. She told me that she was dying and she asked me to stay on and to manage the farm for Mr Heelis when she was gone which I agreed to do. She passed away that night, just three days before Christmas.'

DEATHS
On Wednesday, Dec. 22, 1943 at Castle Cottage, Sawrey, near Ambleside, HELEN BEATRIX, dearly loved wife of WILLIAM HEELIS, and only daughter of the late Rupert Potter. Cremation private. No mourning, no flowers, and no letters, please.

Beatrix was cremated in Blackpool on the last day of the year and her ashes were taken back to Sawrey and scattered on her beloved fells by Tom Storey. 'She asked me to do it but said, "Don't tell anyone where you put them. I want it kept a secret."' And so it has remained. Tom Storey died in March 1986, aged ninety.

Willie was devastated by Beatrix's death and he found it almost impossible to contemplate moving anything of hers from Castle Cottage. He even left a pile of her letters on the table at which he took his meals. Beatrix had appointed him as one of her trustees, together with her brother-in-law George Heelis, Willie's nephew John Heelis of Hawkshead, her cousin Walter Gaddum and her cousin Stephanie's husband, Kenneth Duke. In her will she left nearly everything to Willie for his lifetime, and after his death substantial sums to her cousins, Walter Gaddum and Stephanie Duke. Her shares in Frederick Warne she bequeathed to Norman's nephew, Frederick Warne Stephens, and after Willie's death the rights and royalties in her books were also to come to him. The National Trust were to have over 4,000 acres of her property in the Lake District, including fifteen farms and numerous cottages, and she instructed that the rooms at Hill Top should be kept as she had left them and not to be let to a tenant. The sheep stocks on her fell farms should be maintained of the pure Herdwick breed. A meadow at Satter Howe on the Ferry Hill was to be preserved in memory of the men of Sawrey who fell in the Great War, 1914–18.

Beatrix did not forget her old friends in her will – Miss Woodward in South Kensington, her governesses Annie Moore and

Beatrix Potter died on 22 December 1943. Following her cremation in Blackpool, her ashes were scattered in Sawrey by Tom Storey, seen here driving his cart behind Hill Top.

(*above*) Busk Farm in Little Langdale, under Lingmoor Fell, one of the fifteen farms left to the National Trust by Beatrix in her will.

(*left*) Penny Hill Farm in Eskdale, bought by Beatrix in 1935, another of the farms she left to the National Trust.

Madeline Davidson, and of course Miss Hammond and Miss Mills. Nor did she forget those who had given her faithful service, her housekeeper, Mary Rogerson, her shepherd and farm manager Tom Storey, and her chauffeur Walter Stevens.

Hating all field sports, finally Beatrix declared 'that hunting by otter hounds and harriers shall be forbidden and prohibited over the whole of my Troutbeck property'. To the very end Beatrix was deeply concerned to preserve and protect the natural order.

On the day following the announcement of Beatrix's death *The Times* published a short, factual obituary notice, but the following day Beatrix was the subject of a leading article in the same paper headed 'A Nursery Classic'. After comparing her work to that of Caldecott, Carroll and Grahame, the writer ended on a poignant note: 'Beatrix Potter had died in the days just before Christmas, a time at which, for the last forty years, she has been much in the minds of happy children. It is no mean epitaph, and they are legion who think of her gratefully.'

On 30 December *The Times* printed yet another piece, an appreciation by the portrait painter and an old friend, D. H. Banner. He added a local touch: 'Her many farm tenants all over the dales honoured her as landlord of care and understanding. She was a noted breeder and judge of Herdwick sheep. At all sheep shows could be seen her short, stout, venerable figure, her countenance full of intelligence and humour, her plump, apple-rosy cheeks, and shrewd blue eyes. She was a Cumbrian, solid, realistic, truthful.'

In America Beatrix's death was recorded on 6 January 1944 by the New York *Herald Tribune* in a long editorial which ended: 'Beatrix Potter, North-Country farmer, connoisseur of old furniture and china, lover of nature and animals, was an artist both with words and with brush. The perfect characterisations bear witness to it and are unforgettable. Her greatness lies in the fact that she was able again and again to create that rare thing – a book that brings grown-ups and children together in a shared delight.'

In spite of the attentions of Miss Hammond and Miss Mills, Willie pined for Beatrix, and, as a member of the family recalls, 'He sat mourning until he died himself.' Willie died on 4 August 1945, also leaving his property, some 250 acres of farmland, to the National Trust; the household effects of Castle Cottage he left to Kenneth Duke, 'Confident that he will dispose of them according to my wife's wishes.'

chapter seven

'I have never quite understood the secret
of Peter's perennial charm.'

WHEN MARGARET LANE approached Beatrix Potter in 1941 for permission to write about her she received the most discouraging of replies: 'My books have always sold without advertisement, and I do not propose to go in for that sort of thing now.' One of the articles about Beatrix that appeared in the days following her death bemoaned the fact that so little had been written about her and that 'her name is scarcely to be found in reference books'. From the day of her death, 22 December 1943, that high and hitherto impregnable wall of defence against personal publicity and public acclaim that she had been building all her life lost its most dedicated guardian, and in the following weeks there were more column inches concerning Beatrix Potter in *The Times* than there had been in all the newspapers put together during her long lifetime.

The obituary, the leading article and the appreciation were followed by letters and short news pieces concerning her will and the National Trust well into 1944. Among the letters was one from Cicely M. Barker, the artist of the widely popular *Flower Fairies* books, who suggested that there should be an exhibition of Beatrix Potter's original illustrations. 'They would be a delight to many children, a very great interest to fellow artists, and a pleasure to hundreds of people who have known and loved the little books all their lives. It could also bring in a considerable sum of money for the charities which Beatrix Potter had at heart.'

The following month *The Times* carried a report from one of those charities, the Invalid Children's Aid Association, with an account of how Beatrix had helped them to raise money through the Peter Rabbit Fund, drawing 'several enchanting pictures for Christmas cards' and allowing Peter Rabbit, 'a friend of little children', to be the symbol on their penny stamp collecting cards, which by 1944 had endowed four beds in the Invalid Children's Aid Association Heart Hospital at West Wickham.

In April 1944 Beatrix's name was in *The Times* again. 'The Queen has bought a complete set of Beatrix Potter's "Peter Rabbit" books for children as a sequel to her recent visit to the headquarters of the Red Cross & St John Book Campaign, which the Times Book Club is organising nationally in aid of the Duke of Gloucester's Red Cross & St John Fund.' The countrywide salvage collection of paper for the war effort had resulted in more books being sent off to be pulped than were available for library issue or even for purchase, and a scheme had been set up to collect 'books of sufficient worth to be retained in circulation' which were then sold in aid of the Fund. The books were offered for sale, first to public and county librarians, and then to members of the general public. On her visit to Wigmore Street Queen Elizabeth had bought fifteen volumes from the shelves and then requested the

One of the card designs by Beatrix for the Invalid Children's Aid Association. By 1944 she had helped to raise enough money to endow four beds at the I.C.A.A. Heart Hospital.

Peter Rabbit books, only to be told that none had been donated. As luck would have it, shortly afterwards, a complete set of the little books, in the Peter Rabbit bookshelf with which they were sold at the time, was sent in from Henley-on-Thames and dispatched at once to the Queen.

The name of Beatrix Potter – and of Peter Rabbit – has seldom been out of the news since. In 1946 her beloved Hill Top was opened to the public by the National Trust, with her furniture, her pictures, her ornaments just as she had so carefully arranged and instructed them to be kept. On the back of most pieces there is a note in her writing giving details of its provenance. 'A miniature portrait of a Bartolozzi print? Cut to fit frame. The mutilation is not recent as there is a trace of old houndwork paper at back. Bought at public auction April 25 1908'; and on the back of another picture, 'Mrs Heelis, Esthwaite Mound, bought at Mr W.D. Heelis's sale June 7 1934. 15/-.'

Willie stipulated in his will that the drawings for all Beatrix's books should also 'if possible' be kept at Hill Top, and they were

In 1946 the National Trust
opened Hill Top to the public.
The never-ending stream of
visitors during 'opening times'
makes this a rarely peaceful
view.

indeed displayed there for all-comers to see for nearly forty years.
In that time hundreds of thousands of people, young and old, have
made the pilgrimage to the Potter shrine, so many people that the
very existence of Hill Top is now threatened. The fabric of the
house and the structure of the garden are being eroded by the sheer
force of humanity that flows through the gate from the road, and,
as a National Trust spokesman wrote in 1981, 'with increasing
rapidity the devotees of Beatrix Potter are destroying this spiritual
"home of children" by stripping it of the scale, sensitivity and sympathy which are essential to an appreciation of Beatrix's love of
the countryside, animals and, especially, the Lake District.'

In 1985 the original illustrations were withdrawn from Hill Top 'for conservation' and at the time of writing it is becoming increasingly difficult to see Beatrix's work in its original form. The National Trust have the originals of nearly all the books, the exceptions being those of *The Tale of Peter Rabbit* which are owned by Frederick Warne, *The Tailor of Gloucester*, owned by the Tate Gallery, and *The Tale of the Flopsy Bunnies*, owned by the British Museum. The largest collection of her original paintings and drawings, apart from the books, is the Linder Bequest, which appropriately rests at 'her own' Victoria and Albert Museum as part of the National Art Library. Leslie Linder, the man who cracked the code of Beatrix's journal, and his sister Enid left their entire Potter collection of more than 2,000 items to the museum in 1973, following the Beatrix Potter Christmas Exhibition there. As a known collector and expert, Leslie Linder had been approached to lend items for inclusion and it was his acknowledgement of the care and attention shown by the museum for his material that resulted in his bequest. Most of the items in the collection are too valuable and fragile for exhibition or for general study, but the recently published and meticulously prepared catalogue by Anne Hobbs and Irene Whalley has reproductions of much material that has been seen by few before, and it is a source of delight both for the scholar and for the fan.

Three years before his bequest to the Victoria and Albert Museum, Leslie Linder had given nearly 300 Potter paintings and drawings to the National Book League, after preparing the large 1966 Potter Centenary Exhibition in their headquarters, which were then in central London. Carefully chosen by him to represent the wide range of the artist's work, the Linder Collection was intended for exhibition to the general public and items from it are on permanent display in the Library of Book Trust (the National Book League) now in Wandsworth, not far from the house that Beatrix visited to call on Annie Moore and her children.

Items from both collections have been sent many thousands of miles for exhibition in recent years. In February 1985 fifty pieces from the Linder Collection went to Australia, to be shown in Dromkeen near Melbourne and then in Sydney, and the following month ninety items from the Linder Bequest went to Japan to share an exhibition in five Japanese cities with drawings by Ernest Shepard for the *Winnie-the-Pooh* books. As every year passes, the world-wide interest in Beatrix Potter and her work continues and increases. Fortunately, much of her original work has survived, mostly as a result of her own careful preservation and then distribution. In 1934 she gave an unequalled collection of her watercolours and drawings of fungi, mosses, lichens and fossils to the Armitt Library in Ambleside, together with her archaeological

『ピーター・ラビット』と『クマのプーさん』の世界

ビアトリクス・ポターとアーネスト・シェパードの絵本原画展

In 1985 Beatrix Potter shared an exhibition in Japan with Ernest Shepard, 'The World of *Peter Rabbit* and *Winnie-the-Pooh*'.

watercolours and many of her own and her father's books. The Armitt Library is an old subscription library, founded in 1912 and specialising in books 'of scientific, literary, and antiquarian value ... for the student and book-lover'. Willie Heelis was a trustee of the Armitt, and Beatrix and the Rawnsleys were among its earliest members.

The Perth Museum and Art Gallery also have a fine collection of Beatrix's fungus paintings, an acknowledgement of her debt to Charlie McIntosh with whom she shared her discoveries in Birnam all those years ago. Many of Beatrix's letters to her American friends, and the drawings and paintings that she sent to them or that they acquired over the years, even some of her original manuscripts, have found their way into museum and gallery collections in the United States, including the Free Library of Philadelphia, the Pierpont Morgan Library in New York and the New York Public Library. The letters she wrote to Ivy Hunt (Steel)

'The House of the Tailor of Gloucester' was opened as a Beatrix Potter shop and museum by Warne in 1980.

and to her daughter, June, are in the Osborne Collection in the Toronto Public Library. The list is endless.

In the early 1970s Frederick Warne discovered quite by chance that 9 College Court in Gloucester, drawn by Beatrix as the house of the Tailor of Gloucester, might soon be coming on to the market, but it was not until 1979 that Warne were able to buy it. They restored it to its original condition and then opened the house in 1980 as a Beatrix Potter museum and shop, 'The House of The Tailor of Gloucester', from which is sold the vast range of Beatrix Potter products, from books to pencil sharpeners. The merchandising of the Potter characters, or 'the side-shows' as she called them, begun by Beatrix herself with her Peter Rabbit doll in 1903, the year of the Warne publication of *The Tailor of Gloucester*, has continued unabated ever since. It is now possible to buy a very wide range of Potter products – a Mrs Ribby tea-cosy, a Jemima Puddle-duck jigsaw puzzle, a Tom Kitten face flannel,

The tradition of Potter merchandise, started by Beatrix herself in 1903 with her Peter Rabbit doll, continues apace.

The E.M.I. film *Tales of Beatrix Potter*, made in 1971 and based on 'the little books', is still shown regularly in cinemas and on television.

each item having been carefully overseen at an early stage to ensure that the reproduced image is as faithful to the original as possible.

The sales of the books have also continued – and even increased – since Beatrix's death. Versions in Japanese and Icelandic have joined the long list of translations. The English language editions still bear the publishing imprint of Frederick Warne, although that company was bought by Penguin Books in 1983, and for the first time since its founding by Frederick Warne in July 1865, exactly one year before Beatrix was born, there is no longer a Warne or a Stephens working in the company.

The constant and enduring factor in everything is Beatrix Potter. In recent years she has been the subject of television documentaries and of plays for the theatre. 1971 saw the première of a full-length ballet film, *Tales of Beatrix Potter*, based on her books, and the same characters are frequently used by cartoonists world-wide as inspiration for their lampooning of politicians and public

"A Mr. Squirrel Nutkin and a Mrs. Tiggywinkle are here to see you."

The Beatrix Potter books have been a source of inspiration for cartoonists all over the world. This cartoon (*left*) by Henry Martin, © 1984 The New Yorker Magazine, Inc., was for *The New Yorker* of 13 August 1984.

(*below*) Nicholas Garland, in *The New Statesman* of 11 June 1976, showed Margaret Thatcher, then leader of the Opposition, losing a motion of no-confidence in the James Callaghan government.

215

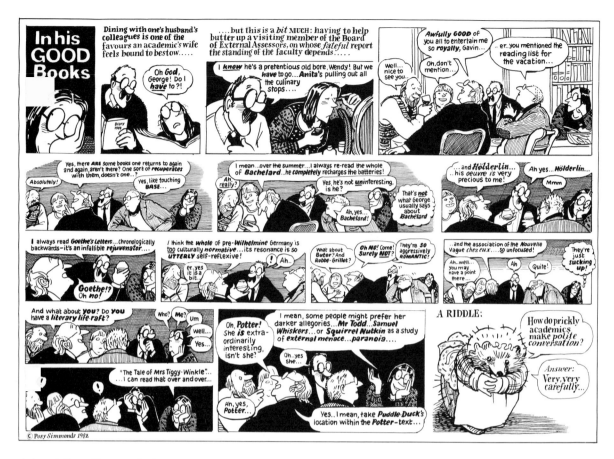

In his GOOD Books

Dining with one's husband's colleagues is one of the favours an academic's wife feels bound to bestow.....

"Oh God, George! Do I have to?!"

....but this is a bit MUCH: having to help butter up a visiting member of the Board of External Assessors, on whose fateful report the standing of the faculty depends.....

"I know he's a pretentious old bore, Wendy! But we have to go...Anita's pulling out all the culinary stops...."

"Awfully GOOD of you all to entertain me so royally, Gavin..."

"Well..nice to see you..."

"Oh..don't mention..."

"er...you mentioned the reading list for the vacation..."

"Yes, there ARE some books one returns to again and again, aren't there? One sort of recuperates with them, doesn't one...?"

"Absolutely!"

"Yes, like touching BASE..."

"I mean...over the summer...I always re-read the whole of Bachelard...he completely recharges the batteries!"

"Ah, really?"

"Yes, he's not uninteresting, is he?"

"Ah, yes... Bachelard!"

"That's not what George usually says about Bachelard"

"...and Hölderlin... his oeuvre is very precious to me!"

"Ah yes... Hölderlin..."

"Mmm"

"I always read Goethe's Letters...chronologically backwards—it's an infallible rejuvenator...."

"Goethe!? Oh no!"

"I think the whole of pre-Wilhelmine Germany is too culturally normative...its resonance is so UTTERLY self-reflexive!"

"er..yes it is a bit."

"! Ah.."

"What about Butor? And Robbe-Grillet?"

"Oh NO! Come! Surely NOT!"

"They're SO aggressively ROMANTIC!"

"...and the association of the Nouvelle Vague chez eux....so unfocused!"

"Ah..well... you may have a point there..."

"Ah"

"Quite!"

"They're just sucking up!"

"And what about you? Do you have a literary life raft?"

"Who?"

"Me?"

"Um well.. Yes..."

"The Tale of Mrs Tiggy-Winkle"... ...I can read that over and over...

"Oh, Potter! She is extraordinarily interesting, isn't she?"

"Ah, yes, Potter..."

"I mean, some people might prefer her darker allegories...Mr Todd...Samuel Whiskers...or Squirrel Nutkin as a study of external menace...paranoia...."

"Oh..yes she..."

"Yes..I mean, take Puddle-Duck's location within the Potter-text..."

A RIDDLE:

"How do prickly academics make polite conversation?"

"Answer: Very, very carefully..."

© Posy Simmonds 1982

(above) Posy Simmonds, in *The Guardian* of 11 November 1982, introduced Beatrix Potter's books into her academics' conversation.

(right) In 1979 the Post Office marked the International Year of the Child with a set of four stamps, designed by Edward Hughes, featuring characters from famous British children's books.

9p

The Tale of Peter Rabbit

figures. In 1979 Peter Rabbit, Jemima Puddle-duck and Squirrel Nutkin were featured on one of the four colourful stamps issued by the Post Office in Britain to mark the International Year of the Child. In 1984 a Beatrix Potter design was included in the UNICEF greeting card selection, and in 1985 the Wildlife Hospitals Trust opened the St Tiggywinkle's Hedgehog Unit at their hospital in Aylesbury, Buckinghamshire, which cares for sick and injured wild animals and birds, particularly the increasing number of hedgehog accident victims.

As well as the thousands of visitors to Hill Top each year, there is a growing number of Potter devotees who go on Beatrix Potter tours to see the places where she lived or where the family went for holidays, but they are sometimes surprised, for things have changed. No. 2 Bolton Gardens, the house where Beatrix was born, has disappeared altogether, having been destroyed by a German landmine on 10 October 1940, and on the site is Bousfield School; Dalguise House in Dunkeld is now owned by the Boys' Brigade of Glasgow and run as a holiday and training centre for young people; Camfield Place is the private home of novelist Barbara Cartland; from Gwaynynog (now Gwaenynog), occupied by a girls' school during the last war, the present descendants of the Burton family make and sell dairy ice cream; the gardens at Lingholm, near Keswick, now the home of Lord Rochdale, are open to the public at certain times; Wray Castle, near Hawkshead, is a training school for Merchant Navy radio operators; and Lindeth How (now Howe), near Windermere, is an hotel.

A drawing by David Austen for *The Spectator* of 31 August 1985.

(*below left*) A two-and-a-half-week-old patient at the St Tiggywinkle's Hedgehog Unit, opened at the Wildlife Hospitals Trust, Aylesbury, Buckinghamshire, in 1985.

(*below right*) The Beatrix Potter Society was founded in 1980 'to promote the study and appreciation of the life and works of Beatrix Potter'.

There are also those whose concern is to continue the tradition of the stories and to preserve the original flavour of the little books. The Beatrix Potter Society was founded in 1980 by a group of people professionally involved in the curatorship of Beatrix Potter material, when they pledged 'to promote the study and appreciation of the life and works of Beatrix Potter'. They publish a quarterly newsletter, hold regular meetings, and promote an annual Linder Memorial Lecture and a biennial study conference. The founders of the society emphasise that Beatrix Potter was not only the author of a classic series of children's books but also a landscape and natural history artist, a diarist, a farmer and a conservationist, which is no doubt just how she would wish to be remembered. Her friend and fellow artist, D. H. Banner, provided the rest. 'No humbug or affectation could approach. She refused to be lionised: and not very many of her unnumbered admirers penetrated her cottage garden, still less her cottage, where old watercolours and silver-mounted guns hung on the walls in the candle and fire light. Her penetrating gaze could alarm the intrusive; but it was those eyes which had observed the creatures that she drew with such a sure hand and such exquisite taste. Her solidity was the basis of her freedom from sentimentality.'

(*below*) Ribby 'sat down before the fire to wait for the little dog'. From *The Tale of the Pie and the Patty-pan*.

Further reading

BATTRICK, ELIZABETH: *The Real World of Beatrix Potter* (A National Trust Pocket Book), Jarrold, 1986.

BROOKE, HENRY: *Leslie Brooke and Johnny Crow*, Frederick Warne, 1982.

CAVALIERO, GLEN (ed.): *Beatrix Potter's Journal* (abridged), Frederick Warne, 1986.

CROUCH, MARCUS: *Beatrix Potter*, The Bodley Head, 1960.

GODDEN, RUMER: *The Tale of the Tales*, Frederick Warne, 1971.

GREENE, GRAHAM: *Collected Essays*, The Bodley Head, 1969.

HOBBS, ANNE STEVENSON and WHALLEY, JOYCE IRENE: *Beatrix Potter: The V & A Collection*, The Victoria and Albert Museum and Frederick Warne, 1985.

KING, ARTHUR and STUART, A. F.: *The House of Warne*, Frederick Warne, 1965.

LANE, MARGARET: *The Magic Years of Beatrix Potter*, Frederick Warne, 1978.

LANE, MARGARET: *The Tale of Beatrix Potter*, Frederick Warne, 1946; revised edition, 1985.

LINDER, LESLIE: *The Art of Beatrix Potter*, Frederick Warne, 1955; revised edition, 1972.

LINDER, LESLIE: *The History of the Tale of Peter Rabbit*, Frederick Warne, 1976

LINDER, LESLIE: *The History of the Writings of Beatrix Potter*, Frederick Warne, 1971.

LINDER, LESLIE: *The Journal of Beatrix Potter*, Frederick Warne, 1966.

MALONEY, MARGARET CRAWFORD (ed.): *Dear Ivy, Dear June: Letters from Beatrix Potter*, Toronto Public Library, 1977.

MILLAIS, JOHN GUILLE: *The Life and Letters of Sir John Everett Millais*, 2 vols, Methuen, 1899.

MITCHELL, W. R.: *Beatrix Potter Remembered*, Dalesman Books, 1987.

MORSE, JANE CROWELL (ed.): *Beatrix Potter's Americans: Selected Letters*, The Horn Book, 1982.

PARKER, ULLA HYDE: *Cousin Beatie*, Frederick Warne, 1981.

RAWNSLEY, ELEANOR F.: *Canon Rawnsley*, Maclehose, Jackson, 1923.

WHALLEY, JOYCE IRENE and BARTLETT, WYNNE K.: *The Derwentwater Sketchbook*, Frederick Warne, 1984.

Acknowledgements

Grateful acknowledgement is made to Graham Greene and The Bodley Head for their kind permission to include the extract from 'Beatrix Potter' in *Collected Essays*, and to the National Trust for extracts from five of Beatrix Potter's letters in their possession. Sincere thanks are due to the following for their kind permission to reproduce the illustrations in this book. Apart from the numbered colour plates, the references given are to the page numbers.

Abbot Hall Art Gallery, Kendal, Cumbria (gift of Mrs Gaddum): 112 (*right*), 113 (*left*)
Beatrix Potter Society, The: 217 (*below right*)
Book Trust, Linder Collection: Plates I, VI, VIII, IX, X, XI, XIII, XV, XVII, XX, XXIV, XXVI, 18, 29, 30, 32 (*above*), 41, 46 (*above and below*), 50 (*left*), 52 (*right*), 58, 62, 76 (*above*), 83, 84, 97, 98, 100, 106, 115 (*left*), 118 (*right*), 124, 125 (*left*), 132, 140 (*left*), 142, 161, 190
Winifred Boultbee: 77 (*left*), 78, 79 (*above and below*), 87, 90, 91, 102, 103, 113 (*right*), 139
J. Brownlow: 202
Mary E. Burkett: 112 (*left*)
Harry Byers: 147 (*above*)
John Clegg: 88, 130, 179, 210
Copyrights: 213
Bryan Dawson: 178
Ina Douglas: 75
Joan Duke: 9, 19 (*right*), 21 (*right and left*), 24, 27, 28, 31 (*left*), 38 (*above and below*), 39, 40, 48 (*above*), 50 (*right*), 53, 54 (*right*), 57, 63 (*above and below*), 77 (*right*), 111, 119,
120, 121 (*above*), 127, 131, 173, 197, 201, 204
E.M.I.: 214
M. C. Fair: 148
Free Library of Philadelphia, Rare Book Department: 68
Nicholas Garland: 215 (*below*)
Girl Guides Association: 165
Betty S. Hart: 93, 162, 185 (*left*), 187, 200 (*above*)
John Heelis: 128 (*below*), 129, 135, 146, 183 (*left*), 191
Jean Holland: 19 (*left*), 51, 108, 175, 180, 183 (*right*), 184, 196
The Horn Book Magazine: 185 (*left*), 198
Richard Hough: 26 (*below*), 48 (*below*), 96 (*below*), 141
Hulton Picture Library: 12 (*below right and left*), 14, 136
Robert B. Hutton: 64 (*right*)
Imperial War Museum: 195
Japan Art and Culture Association: 211
David W. Jones: 109, 157 (*and insert*), 172, 186, 192, 205 (*above and below*)
Manchester Public Libraries, Local History Library: 13
Marjorie Moore: 54 (*left*)
National Art Library, Victoria and Albert Museum, Leslie Linder Bequest: Plates III, IV, V, VII, XII, XIV, XVI, XIX, XXI, XXII, XXIII, XXVIII, 10, 15, 17, 20, 22, 25, 26 (*above*), 32 (*below*), 33, 36, 37 (*left*), 42, 43, 44, 45 (*above and below*), 47, 49, 52 (*left*), 56, 59 (*above*), 64 (*left*), 66 (*above*), 67 (*below*), 70, 71, 73 (*below*), 81, 82, 85, 89, 94 (*right*), 95 (*below*), 99 (*above*), 104 (*left*), 107 (*below*), 116, 117 (*right and left*), 128 (*above*), 140 (*right*), 143 (*left*), 149, 152, 154 (*left*), 155, 159, 160, 164 (*left*),
168, 171 (*left*), 174, 176, 181, 185 (*right*), 189, 199 (*below*)
National Portrait Gallery: 23
The National Trust: 16, 34, 147 (*below*), 155, 200 (*below*)
New York Public Library, Rare Books and Manuscripts Division, Anne Carroll Moore Collection: 153, 177
The New Yorker: 215 (*above*)
E. E. Oliver: 11 (*below*), 12 (*above*)
Parker, Sir Richard Hyde: 193
Perth Museum and Art Gallery: 59 (*below*), 60
Photo Source: 188
Post Office: 216 (*below*)
Rosalind Rawnsley: 69
Louisa Rhodes: 144, 167 (*above*)
Posy Simmonds: 216 (*above*)
Tom Smith: 65
The Spectator: 216 (*above*)
Les Stocker: 217 (*below left*)
Joan Thornely: 166
Times Newspapers: 138
Topham: 126, 158 (*above*)
Frederick Warne: Plates II, XVIII, XXV, XXVII, 1, 4, 6, 8, 11 (*above*), 31 (*right*), 35, 37 (*right*), 55, 61, 66 (*below*), 67 (*above*), 72, 73 (*above*), 76 (*below*), 86 (*above and below*), 92 (*above and below*), 94 (*left*), 95 (*above*), 96 (*above*), 99 (*below*), 101, 104 (*right*), 105, 107 (*left and right above*), 110, 114, 115 (*right*), 118 (*left*), 121 (*below*), 122 (*above and below*), 123, 125 (*right*), 133 (*above and below*), 134, 141, 143 (*right*), 145, 148, 150, 151, 154 (*right*), 158 (*below*), 163, 164 (*right*), 167 (*below*), 169, 170 (*above and below*), 171 (*right*), 193, 194, 199 (*above*), 203, 207, 209, 212, 213, 217 (*below right*), 218, 219

Index

Beatrix Potter's name is abbreviated to BP